FIREBREAKS

FIREBREAKS

POEMS

JOHN KINSELLA

W. W. NORTON & COMPANY

INDEPENDENT PUBLISHERS SINCE 1923

NEW YORK   LONDON

For information about permission to reproduce selections from this book,
write to Permissions, W. W. Norton & Company, Inc.,
500 Fifth Avenue, New York, NY 10110

For information about special discounts for bulk purchases, please contact
W. W. Norton Special Sales at specialsales@wwnorton.com or 800-233-4830

Manufacturing by Quad Graphics
Book design by JAM Design
Production manager: Louise Mattarelliano

Library of Congress Cataloging-in-Publication Data

Names: Kinsella, John, 1963– author.
Title: Firebreaks : poems / JOHN KINSELLA.
Description: New York : W. W. Norton & Company, [2016]
Identifiers: LCCN 2015043965 | ISBN 9780393352610 (pbk.)
Classification: LCC PR9619.3.K55 A6 2016 | DDC 821/.914—dc23 LC record available at
http://lccn.loc.gov/2015043965

W. W. Norton & Company, Inc.
500 Fifth Avenue, New York, N.Y. 10110
www.wwnorton.com

W. W. Norton & Company Ltd.
Castle House, 75/76 Wells Street, London W1T 3QT

1 2 3 4 5 6 7 8 9 0

TO TRACY AND TIM

The author wishes to acknowledge the traditional owners and custodians of the land he writes.

CONTENTS

INSIDE OUT

from Jam Tree Gully/Coondle in the time of 'mouse plague' and fire

on Mizen Peninsula, Ireland

Jam Tree Gully Envoys

ACKNOWLEDGMENTS

Australian Book Review
Boston Review
Colorado Review
Griffith Review
Literary Imagination
New Statesman
Outcrop: Radical Australian
  poetry of land (ed. Bailus
  and Wakeling)
Overland
Poem
Poetry
Poetry London

Privacy Policy: The Anthology
  of Surveillance Poetics
  (ed. Andrew Ridker)
Salmagundi
Southerly
The Australian
The Best Australian Poetry 2013
The Best Australian Poetry 2014
The Common
The Hampden–Sydney Poetry Review
The Iowa Review
The Kenyon Review
Westerly

Thanks to my editor Jill Bialosky, to my partner Tracy Ryan, to the various editors of the journals and anthologies listed above, and to Tom Bristow, David Brooks, Philip Mead and others who have discussed this manuscript with me over the last couple of years. I also wish to acknowledge the (frequently oppositional) dialogue I've had with Ovid's late works of exile, *Tristia* and *Ex Ponto*, and Gaston Bachelard's *The Poetics of Space* and *The Psychoanalysis of Fire*.

FIREBREAKS

INTERNAL

EXILE

PROLOGUE: SCAN

(JUST BEFORE LEAVING JAM TREE GULLY)

It's not an inspection or reconnoitre
but a scan of the block: on the eve of solstice
and feeling 'fluey', the day disturbingly blue
and new flakes and chips off the granites, shelled
by cold, having reached the limits of expansion
during a tragic summer. Sundered — not impelled
or compelled or driven — to scan hillside, to see
what change scant rain that fell so quick and hard
has brought since last week, the cold, the high winds
that swept in and continue to sweep eastwards.
Revelations — not observations or details or facts —
of what I've come across and encountered and experienced
include: new beds of moss, branches and whole trees
scuttled, no belated revival of those lost in summer:
but far-reaching echidna diggings whose orbits
are growing *wider*, concentric circles wobbling
out to boundaries, shorelines of valley,
echidna seeming to know better than us,
though this might shift with a follow-up scan,
packaging data to fit the model — thus, *revelation*.
And the run-off from toproad and hillcrest
washes sands and stones I didn't really know
were part of the soil profile, gathering leaves and rubbish
from curved space: even a beer can from a distant
neighbour's party-site, and a flower pot
with the name of an exotic European herb
written around its belly in black indelible ink,
but empty of all contents, a strainer for air.

And a new bullant nest so massive I have no idea
how it was engineered with such rapidity, unless
it has been cloaked from every scan I've cast —
hundreds and hundreds carried out in all conditions
inside and out of me, on shortest or longest days,
whether wrecked by storms or becalmed.

ENGLISH EXILE

TO WHOM AM I WRITING?

Monitors and geckoes?

Rally organisers?

Wedge-tailed eagles & their offspring (past, present, yet to hatch)?

Red-capped robins?

Barn owl?

The Red Shed?

Skinks?

Jam tree saplings hedging the crossover?

Neighbours?

Specifically the young fellas with guns and a home-made cannon?

Aberration?

Contradiction?

Toodyay stone?

York gums hollowed and vulnerable in high winds?

Panorama?

Elevation?

Mosquitoes and their larvae?

The lack of water?

Erosion?

The residue of an aggressive visitor, hell-bent on vengeance with little or no
    grounds?

Roos and/or euros?

Sandalwood?

Echidna, echidnas, echidnae?

Gravel?

Granite boulders emitting low-level radiation and hosting lichen?

Lichen?

Moss?

Wild oats broken or resting as seed on dry earth?

Storms?

Books gathered from around the world, waiting?

The idea of trespass?

The absence of owners?

Possession?

Exclusion?

Twenty-eight parrot in the hollow of a tree?

History of fire?

Ice on the windows as dawn imposes?

The crack of metal expanding in transformative heat?

Honeyeaters at a crack in the tank, siphoning traces of moisture?

The story itself?

You all?

Us?

It.

IN CAMBRIDGE I STAY UP INTO
THE EARLY HOURS

I stay up into the early hours to morph
Jam Tree Gully time, that sick lag
sharpening senses before they quit
entirely, taking memory of granite

and red-capped robins, eagles and lichen
bruised and transformed by the sun,
away with them. Silver birches
and coal tits negotiate thin space

and dunnocks frenzy in yew.
I see them from a walk earlier
with Tim, who is acclimatising
to these flatlands, the draining.

I stay up into the early hours to morph
into Jam Tree Gully time, walk as John
walks caretaking from York, a journey
in itself, but of one and the same time.

HOWLING WIND, CAMBRIDGE

The wind howls around the Sheppard Flats
And I am in Jam Tree Gully, but grateful
It's the cold Atlantic winds cutting across
A winter island and not the hot winds
Of the summer it is down there which
Would bring the fear of inferno. Here
The wind passes almost freely through
Leafless trees; down there the volatile
Leaves of the eucalypt would be drawn
To low pressure, snapping the spine
Of their evergreen anatomies. That's
The rub of exile, the pain of absence
But the relief in some small ways as well,
The lessening of anxiety that is its own
Anxiety; here at night I also hear an owl.

BOUND BY PROPERTIES

The wind is still blasting the fens.
It rolls and gathers momentum.
It incites peat to dry and crumble
to dust where it pokes its head
out of the wet. It makes for a violence
of opposites. And it compels my
vicarious steps through memory,
rewiring the vascular emphasis
of trees struggling in heat at Jam Tree
Gully; a whiplash circuitry where
sun solders rock and cellulose,
as it welds heavy cloud and sharp
cold here, swept away, and yet
staining. The properties of weather
undo all owning, all claims, all
junk bonds and derivatives,
all old poems claiming electric
links through wild-flowers, those
reactors gently leaking and smiling
the other way, castigating seeds
carried at high altitudes around
the globe. Compressed in thought,
it is still a long way away, so far apart.
The wind is still blasting the fens.

SLEEPY HOLLOW TRANSPOSITIONS INCLUDING A SIX-LINE STANZA (INCARNATIONS OF JAM TREE GULLY RECOLLECTED FROM ENGLAND)

Left, it will revert *not* to picture.
The wild is incursion that will only
manifest in weeds, insects and fire.
Cats will increase their patrols
and small skulls will start dead lives.

When we arrived, there were skulls
of large animals – *beasts* – mounted
on the gate. The fruits of decapitations
before or after death, depending
on where death begins and ends.

But the trophies were taken down
and laid to rest. No longer warnings
to enemies, who weren't put off,
but attracted. Like St Francis,
folk there speak to the animals,

but every line is end-stopped
with human. Where granites
and gnarled trees and thin topsoil
and water dragged from deep down
make surface, animals wait.

I miss their waiting. I miss
comforting. Indifference isn't tough
or philosophical or intellectually

rigorous. Listen to rustling, chewing,
trilling, rubbing, clashes, calls, embraces.

At least we made it a place of the living.
Translation had some leeway it required.
We replaced the punctuation of guns.
Parataxis was just syntax: splice
and overlay of all speech.

Now, away from this earliest
of stories, disappeared into a distance
outside physics, I elicit Washington Irving's
description of an 'Indian summer': 'serene
but somewhat arid', like all insensitivity
we conjure as landscape. Sun burns

Sleepy Hollow as much as Jam Tree Gully,
into memory's skin – both deleterious, cancer-
causing, but both as different as the shifts
to death we make with our living. Once,
here, it was called St Martin's Summer,

but that was for an earlier world,
with earlier grammars of weather? Then,
as now, the red of robins in all places:
different species, maybe, though still
delicate-skulled prophets, not trophies.

THE GURU KEEPS AN EYE ON
JAM TREE GULLY IN OUR ABSENCE

The guru is staggering saplings
below firebreaks alongside
the gravel strip grammatically
informing the house. Meticulous.
We know without being there.
Gurus expect trust, emphatic
belief, faith in destinations.

The guru knows jam trees
are planted with sandalwood.
He knows ants have made their way
up the curlicue of poly-pipe
into the water tank. They carry
moisture and body parts
of gnats in their pincers.

The guru follows the roo trails:
droppings, tail swatches on dusty
ground. He counts the blessings
of eagles whose shadows swallow
him whole. He relives the moment
in telling. No moment stands alone.
All is narrative. All is necessary.

The guru is a master of irony.
But he doesn't slacken his pace.
The hill steepens or levels

as needs be: he plays gradients
like luck, but denies luck its part.
He reads the tracks of strangers
pretending to visit.

BLOCKING OUT (THE HOME SCHEDULE)

Trees are going into hard ground.
Crowbar and pick-axe prise open
to inlay saplings with protective
coverings to mesh into a greater
protective covering to ward off androids,
to keep the greedy out or delude us – me –
into thinking they'll stay away, to inlay shadow
and parabola sun, to insulate against headlong
crashes into the centrifuge of tranquillity,
to screen drifts of generation on generation
of stronger poisons, the anxiety and paranoia
of food-growth, of capital-making (it
is accumulation, it *is* power, it *is* proto-
typical) to smash down barter and offering,
cast violent gestures at ants and dragonflies,
carnivorous birds and reptiles
distending the grotesque in ways
imagined or denied by those
closed out; wanting in,
wanting in.

THE MENTAL BARRIERS TO HOME

The mansion on the hilltop looks down at all we are,
surveying and watching, a far-gazing grab for attention.

The rally organisers thwarted last year are eyeing off
the loop again. They must rise up from the dust and claim.

Who will stop erosion once erosion has set in?
Who will interdict hunters chasing roos across the block?

I want to move to where the Pyrenees meet the Mediterranean
because it is hot and dry and mountains work as contrast

or anathema, because we know anathema is part of a life.
Wildfires run through there and a species of poisonous snake.

We will be vigilant but comprehend the risks, the eviscerating
winds that change moods and lead to mistakes and damage.

We will be wary because it's already part of our vocabulary.
My letters will be the letters of the requited who casts

himself as unrequited, dust so ingrained in his pores
whole oceans can't wash it away. I will fall to similes, I hope.

That's the plan, to explore mental barriers to home.

PHOTO OF AN EAGLE AT JAM TREE GULLY SENT TO US AT CAMBRIDGE

Eagle framed in blue,
vivid light and dark at once,
overlays an image true
to one you stored as tenant

below sky it inhabits.
Just blueness and eagle,
and yet you know its traits,
position on chart and all

it implicates on hills below:
generation of mice to glean,
small birds bound to nests, slow
rabbits dazzled by absent sun

and illness. I know each degree,
each arc, every pixel of sky. While
there – *home* – I looked intently
up as much as down, and I call

those navigations' escrow.
Eagle's beak will ingress
north, and then as now,
in its wake, cloud will coalesce.

REPORT FROM JAM TREE GULLY

John's report has come in: despite
summer, a wet spring and heatwave storms
mean York gum saplings are thrusting up all over
to match jam tree saplings up by the top
gate, and bees are thick in creeper
flowering beyond its usual range,
by the front door of the house.
He has laid extra slabs across
yellow sand to the gravel drive,
a winter luxury when sludge sticks
to boots and shoes. But roo-prints
will still show up alongside, setting
over dry days and casting topographies.
I have a feeling of elation. Even the burnt
area of a neighbouring paddock brings relief:
they burnt in spring rather than poisoned —
though bringing its problems, it's not
the same realm of hurt. But the crash
comes as I process images he's sent,
photos of pressure that are as local
and specific as eddies in streams
cut through the block after
stormburst. Nothing is benign.
To paint its depth create
a canvas both naïve and redolent
with symbolism. Soutine would have
it all bending and warping into the easterly,
no matter how much he loved. Knowing
that even brilliant red flowerings,
brilliant red markings on birds,

would look like blood from outside:
what they want from us, what they'll
drain to last drops to feed
reasons for living, a need to feed.
John ignores these threats when he's there:
for him it's a constant celebration
of living, working with what's at hand.

FIG TREE, JAM TREE GULLY

Among self-sown native saplings
it's all about what you become:
how many figs you bear
and for how long.

You began as a seedling
in a pot and unleaved abruptly
when winter kicked in. We were
with you then. You looked dead.

We left you like that.
And now, planted out
by another's hand, you
thrive. Hot weather

can't keep you back, and well-
watered, you stand out.
It's a different green
leaves inflect.

If we ever return
it will be when you
are fruiting. Maybe not
first fruits, but all things

being equal, an earlier
than later fruiting,
in what we hope
will be long life

surrounded by native trees
which will work with you
to survive, flourish,
fit in and make new light.

RETURN

TO JAM TREE GULLY:

INTERNAL EXILE

MIXING THE REGISTERS

It's philosophy to state the first twenty-eight
You see is vertical in a poison-shocked tree
In the blank grey of roadside elimination:
And you heard it before you saw it, an off-centre
Calling to a lost mate, to a spoiled horizon.
Following its gaze out where there are no
First times and lines run on to feign the infinite.

Here, so much is finite, and the trace
Destabilises images as hefty four-wheel drives
Are dusty before they get to the red north, to new
Fields of uranium, once ancient and quiet.

On entering The Loop and seeing a sign
Announcing forthcoming 'road closures',
The motor sports enthusiasts victorious
In your absence, a proxy long-distance protest
Lodging on nothing, the reckless cars
Will barge through to hasten the dying-off.

Welcome home; bare bones of class
And hunger. What can you say to vested
Interests? Fewer parrots to hear now,
To see chatting on even half-healthy limbs.

As if they have a right. But the last sandal-
Woods are being grubbed out by the greedy,
And would have been, in truth, even if you'd
Stuck around nurturing the attachment
Of a few strays to older and steadier rhizomes,

The dogs of town colloquially rooting in the street
Or watching on, weird laws intervening

Like buckets of water in a slow, dry winter.
For some laws work better than others,
And George Orwell was a spy who ratted
On the those of the Left he suspected.

Dead land. Worn to the bone, burnt
     down past the cellular. They're coming,
and they've been, preparing, burning out
     echidnas from hollows at the end of summer,
preparing their spectacular: high-octane
     euphemistic tongue out in the face of ruin.
The *ten-second rule* of life, the *ten-second rule*
     of tinpot despots. They've murdered bullocks,
stoned their fields, driven horses into circuses.
     Who will listen to me, wife? I was white-
haired early. How much I brought it down
     on myself told by lengths of these lines.
Careful planning for damnation. Redrafting
     of one's birth certificate a contract
little to do with self. I did see a young roo
     in the halflight, just after discovering
the excoriation of the reserve, the burning
     of its corpse. It was halfway downhill,
eyeing off grass growing where trees had stood.
     Caught in the paradox of belonging
as much or more than ourselves. Home,
     the most intense exile? They profit
from your days, the offer of a resting place,
     space as temporary as the sandalwoods
lacking hosts, those last vestiges crisped
     and dampened. There are few beginnings
left in those ends. And why go back there?

REPLY

to *Ex Ponto* IV, 15

I do not want to leave this land
and yet feel I must.

They have destroyed
its equilibrium.

Don't tell them I've returned,
though I write begging
for news of what's left behind.

The poultice. The sting.

I do not want to return
And yet I feel I must.

Paradox of hillside
and ravine.

Limping marsupial
mouse.

Ragged pink-and-greys
in dead branches.

The burning-out.

I do not want to leave this land
And yet feel I must.

CONFRONTATION WITH THE NEW
REALITY & LISTENING TO
7 YEAR BITCH'S "SICK 'EM"

No begging letters to realtors who advertise
two hundred acres of bush paradise
as nature reserve like no other
but one with mining lease available
on application if you want to swing
in the other direction: property for all
seasons. No begging letters to gunsmiths
to protect our lives from expansionist
rimfiring, rage to centrefire proxy
to show love to all beasts and fellows.
No, not interested in their blood tests
at distant medical stations (cutbacks
to apportion reserves where most needed);
bush-ranger image make-over self-
identification, this local version of melting pot
where 'scum' is skimmed off, rottweiler
pitbull shaved-headed tattoo claims
square peg round shit money under table
or a bottle of Jacks hot fuck red revvers
the new freedom, mirror images of Eureka
stockade ganja smoke out the chimney
rejection of *gay shit*. To find humanity
within or not humanity at all? Rather
it be tree sap (that's me, gay as tree sap),
or unpulverised granite declension,
dabbling with beginnings to suture
an end, skinbags we're made into,
in your face (or mine) as they party

hard. All their guns, they got guns,
all their guns, got 'em guns, crack
to alarm the dawn or evening calling
card, countrified deadshells of cars,
rust of a fortnight on and a fortnight
off the mines, in bed with big eaters
and their servants: girls ministering,
the Queen they bow down to, guns,
all guns and epaulettes and bayonets,
to be loved by metal as fine as string
through eyes of steel fenceposts.
No begging letters to master owners:
just a riot, just a fucking riot!

Come here, join the protest.
Gather here while ye may.

Writing the pretty birds
without wondering where
and how they might nest.

No point looking to region,
for assuredly none will arrive.

From Wongan Hills with its dirt
car race track and corroding
nature reserves, from Northam
with its 'sink the boats' racists?

Do racists and ecological nihilists
segue? What of those nationalists
who are selective gumtree advocates?
Never only by name and symbol.
From other towns in the Avon Valley.
A set of seven waves at the stormface?
Alternative lifestylers thinly spread,
and their local produce to look after, too?
Or the city where a handful
of ageing anarchists dwell?
Carousing in anger and bliss.
Sleeping as lead shipments
sail out of the port, where
bohemia has its happy enclave.
Or suburban anonymity?

Some are smart, some beautiful,
some dedicated, some radical.
Some will risk losing all they have.

Anti-nuke port with nuclear
ships just off shore, skulking
underwater to the Babylonian
island. The woosh of launch,
if not the final impact.

Radiation and that bewildering
cry of the hungry seagull.
Occasionally its type
will stray inland.

Dust gathering in the house
leaves no footprints
and yet we slave away
cleaning inside out.

The first weebill I see
clings to a wattle
buffeted by wind. It flits,
headfirst, into a cold easterly,
its 'master'. All that protest,
all those tenuous moments,
near and far.

CORRIDOR

A long central corridor runs through this house —
a backbone. But it's only a comparison,
and a poor one at that.

This place is all exo-skeleton, and the corridor
is a digestive tract, the walls of the house
a kind of membrane, a lining.

It is the hill the house rests on that's the body,
and being part of a greater body it naturally gels
and wrestles with its parent.

The body is sick.
A definite article.

GRUBBING OUT *SOLANUM NIGRUM* AND IMAGINING HACKING OUT *ATROPA BELLADONNA* WITH A HOE

Return is the profligacy of the deadly,
or witness of excess taken root in absence:
the spread and rapid growth in areas
where there'd been no sign of *infestation*.
So deadly, so *belle laide*, warped shades
of green, then green to black-hearted berries,
to hack out hallucinatory from block's
ochre flesh in damper spots, under cover
of great bent eucalypts and moisture-trapping
boulders, a cloud of poison accompanying
dark dreams and flying spells.

But the misattribution is a cautionary
tale in so many ways: fact is, this is blackberry
nightshade, one of the world's most common weeds,
and its toxicity is debatable or at least finely
timed in its cycle. Neighbours scour roadsides
and warn of death to come, though there
are rumours of a tasty if deceptive jam.
Still, there's at least one specimen
of *atropa belladonna* in a Tasmanian herb-
arium, and its influence spreads through sleep.

To hack out down past taproot, gather starburst
flowers and juicy, globular berries, to remove
entirely then gently cover up the wounded ground,
though so many seeds have fallen already,
spread via the guts of animals and birds

enamoured of doors of perception,
disappointedly shitting out their fates,
but living their visions nonetheless.

ON FIRST LOOKING BACK INTO
JAM TREE GULLY

Returning after too much travelling, you notice
what's gone, and you'll notice more that's gone
later, on a bright winter's day, though failing sight
and pale evening light skew the picture.
The word *discovery* might work here.
Even 'eureka': the better side of science?

So, against the violence of shire and 'motor
sports enthusiasts', a silence clings to valley:
two boomers launch from a gravel road
into the gully's throat, playing confluences,
this six-acre compression little hope of sustaining
after the many acres of reserve have been wrecked.

Change came faster than we imagined,
a year to turn the clockspring to snapping.
But on ground left bare in the *adjustment*,
enough lifts to say, 'Some things are reversible,
up to a point.' Hey, I even thought I glimpsed
a trio of parrots in deadwood, one of which

was long thought extinct. I offer no proof.
Decide what you will do about this. Decide.

A DAY IN THE LIFE

1.

The extent of echidna diggings
over the block is astonishing —
a turning-over, an excavation,
a grand furrowing. A fungus corona
around a bare spot with green
winter grass fringing.

2.

The green peak of hill
with the brown house atop
will be orange and dead red
in coming weeks. Too lazy to cut grass,
the sprayman cometh to the neighbour's
spread. We breathe
their work ethic.

3.

The fireman says over the phone:
we lost some timber. Me: the great flooded gums
at the base of the valley? Yes. Full of fuel,
upright for three days then crash! You weren't around,
he adds, so we couldn't get in through your place
to burn the last pocket of bush. Next year.
We'll see about that. We'll see. Plan ahead.

4.

I refuse to read the news today:
I am writing it. Local. Up-close fatalism.

5.

Winter sun shone sharp,
radiating through blue atmosphere;
a small reptile appeared suddenly
on a rock but vanished
before it could be identified.
Though it knew itself. And the nature
of the odd conditions?

6.

Spark in the chamber
day reloads. Metaphor
works literally.
Friday night.
They will fire
all their guns.

7.

Ash in the air
chimneyed up
from the V,
over the fleshy rim.
Holds onto sunset
preternaturally.
Ash in the gutters,
our water, trepanned
from the scarred rooves
of house and shed.

ASHES TO ASHES

The Big Burn here forty years prior
Ogles new pyromania. Just spot fires,
He says, All that dead stuff, bark strips
Hanging high overhead, up to the canopy
Of flooded gums too thick for loving couples
Hand-in-hand to reach around: how many
Kelvins? Enough energy to light the district.
Where water now collects, the great sap
Of the earth suckers the dead and gone,
Those inward-collapsing chimney trunks.
Imploded habitat. You couldn't begin
To count lifeforms in just *one* of those trees.
I taste the ashes; my return is ash and poison:
Dead hilltops, dead valley, and the gully
Of neutrality a conduit between two
Extinctions. Today I cleaned the fireplace.
Ash a year old and new ash from a week
Returned: all that storm-fallen wood,
Old fenceposts whose treatments long
Wore off, but only cut to the soil-line
Anyway. I empty ashes into a steel bucket
And convey them to the heap. A gentle
Breeze picks the upper layers and mixes,
It mixes with all that's lost, each particle
A variable for time to play with, have its way.

ENGINES INDUCE ANXIETY

As evening unsettles with cloud
nipping into the sun, not even
a glimpse of orange, just a shroud
of purple bruising on the crown

of the hills, distant engines
catch in my lungs, their growling
a pulmonary endgame, a sign
of category error or brooding

embolism. The high-pitched
or low-pitched, the whirr
and toothy rev catechised
rip into pits of faith, the stir

of optimism when they fade
lost as another engine registers
its claim on us. Where they're made,
what chemistry feeds their

purpose: drag, pull, lift, draw,
saw, bite, grab, church, levitate,
an early or late ploy to score
more space, repress the irate

and the anxious, plastic tape
woven through fences marking
the route of an engine coup,
where time will fall to time-keepers

and engines roar into view,
birds struck dead on the road
or lifting or mid-air, a curfew
on day and night impressed, stressed.

STONE HEROES

Which myths you latch onto, quickly   or which stone you might build from
while shoring up those defences   all of it about conflict

even the sign up on the gate   keep out you are not wanted
and this is about place real place   with its attitudes and claims
imposition of the body   reading it as DNA
(and who got the prize claiming that?)   right down to petite birdcall

sans place sans land sans scape sans here   and now that hesitation
to flag to cairn to resurrect   weight of worship imposing
or imposition foundations   for whom noticed by and when
a lapse or continental drift   bridge collapses echoes rebirths

to say I don't know is potent   regress of one's own downfall
as when the right protests their 'right'   to suppress and inflict *help*
where less is more red-capped robin   roars its little nest space left
fundamental as a tree down   in your yard your paddock your

claim to replay rockhound childhoods   flying past on winged sandals
myth-mash retort of scorpions   on slab of bark here and now
in Faustian intertitles   so abecedarian
a messiah steps the hot rocks   so the water carrier
embraces drought AND his lone source: 'get what you can out of it!'
but don't enjoy the scents and tastes   of weeds occluding THEIR weeds

with such growth amidst stone heroes   a Hepworth garden forming
what imperceptible object   takes claims into tribunals
of burnt light's white-hot conviction   from a desired sinecure?
What force worthy outside senses   and the affliction of roads.

To make as barren olive trees   brambles and pasture: grazing
less salubrious for exiles   buy-in new colonials
shall only keep their feet planted   exclusionary wilding
reduced to measuring your plot   with balls of string, hankering.

INTERROGATION DEMOTICS
(TO OVID IN EXILE)

1.

Who questions whom?

2.

I don't often handwrite
letters these days
but when I do it's reflex
action: but don't send seed
or sand in reply.
Pasteurise.

3.

Inside outside in.
Roman tragedy.
Forcing as much grain
into and out of the dirt
as conceivable. Costing.

4.

The town doctor (of twenty years)
suddenly unsupported by monetarily
and ethically challenged councillors
now practises in Wongan Hills
where support was proffered.

Many of his patients travel
an hour to see him in his exile

where new roots turn exile
on its head: etymologically
and geographically re-fanged.

5.

To depart on your own terms
is not to return on the same terms.

A liquid metal glint out of drought-ravaged trees
offset by anxious bird-shifts (an unresolved
halfway song) distracts.

Investigate and report.

Took half-an-hour to get back to this space of the page
as much hint as you want it to be, calibrating
according to style
of reading, wilfulness of comprehension: steel posts, lines of wire.

6.

Stringing out possession. Claims.

In appellation is default: features deleted, killing off
the roadside vegetal worlds. Storms with great breakers
of sludge, the barrelling furrows. Who would survive
heading out to the wastes, to the marginal
libraries?

When cast-down trees sucker they'll knock them over.
Lingua franca of appellants. The monuments of conquest: the
    bullet-ridden
road signs, foxes impaled on posts. Momentum

leaves you as chaff to their toxic breeze.
Time is a con. We've no part in it.
Fibre-optic cable and satellites draw
us no closer.

7.

Apprehension in the distorting mirror
of homecoming: post-partum reflection,
crucible in the kiln. How much of a let-down
might your return have been,
so intoxicated by the lack,
the brutality of outcome: Princess and the pea,
the slight, the *inconsolable* outcome?
And enemies who might hear
of letters written, piling up, unsent.

Fealty is the bull in the pasture
down on the corner where alpacas
might fail to protect whose flocks?
Slavery in its many forms.

8.

Wave motion unification (*ex ponto*)
        to claim proper conduct of recollection: I know
that raging face, those crazed limbs: breakdown
        spoliation, that close relation,
to trash the vista and agitate sleep arrangements;
        speculation songs, by-law plays
and pay-offs, and threats: ring-necked parrots
        too heavy for damaged hills, can't gain
enough lift (though svelte and delicate), yet still too

64

robust, incinerated after first flush of green,
their rude tongues increasingly lapidary, formalist.

9.

I string it out along the fence, Ovid, and eye bare spaces
          and think if there's one thing that's useful
from a New Physics it's an affirmation that it's a crowded
          universe and we should negotiate this: what passes
through us, what is blocked, what is deflected attracted confused.
          The patch not burnt-out is thin on vegetation
but the echidnas and so much else dwell there: maybe
          I can work a deal: for all the wanton destruction
this patch dedicated to exclusion: solely an animal and plant
world. Beyond profit and entertainment. A myth generator
          Hope.

10.

I feel most secure
when the sun is down
over the hills
but likely still glinting
on the coastal plain.
It is my leitmotif.
The shire workers
have ceased their butchery
(under orders), parties
haven't begun across
the valley. The guns
are restless in cabinets,
under rugs, a few beers
away . . . dinner almost

on the table. The in-between
birds make a quiet fuss,
frantic but cautious.
I hear you.
I hear you.

11.

Or in pitch-black
absence of moon
and stars blocked-out
dead forests sprout,
dense with animals,
though you stagger
in all directions
without bumping
into anything.

12.

Only the same letters
will get written from here.
And few delivered.

'et Getico scripsi sermone libellum'
        Ovid

'The failure of my lines'
       trimming back and tidying,
             writing in the demotic
of fire officers
       and road-makers,
             wondering what it's like
from the air-cushioned seat
       as dust filters
             into the cab,
blade down to slice
       the shoulder.
             In praise
of shire president, to make
       me one of them? Fuck off!
             I sign my name
to this bitterness,
       not pretend
             it's someone else,
or pretend
       I am pretending
             when I am not.
This is what I want:
       to set what they say
             to my own beat,

a more familiar beat
than you might think:
I am all of my past,
and more. Who says, 'It's what
the community want,
it's good for Toodyay'?

POSITIVE MARKERS

Pink-and-greys watch in clusters,
a wagtail plays the gambit;
all are interested in my effort
to unearth a positive marker.

The marker is a subdivision;
the marker is the state's conviction.
But a cry of 'found it!' or 'eureka!'
enables the galahs a future.

Such a paradox is not resolved,
and a marker lost opens ground
to punishment: the wagtail,
out of character we're told, fails

to see the joke: a survey
desecrates and conveys
against hypotenuse, the stretch
of hillside we inhabit, a sketch

of granites and suckering dead-
trees, and a sky held in charred
arms, an insect world where flitting birds
digest arithmetic: this absurd

psalter of prayers and days,
great works of proof, rays
of GPS allotting portions of the range,
rendering my efforts mute and strange.

SOME PARTS OF LANGUAGE

Some parts of language
fall into silence or die here:
what makes language
or imagines it necessary.

That's what I am trying to grow through;
displaced heritage, land-grabbing of the endemic,
theft of Ballardong place-words.

I can see Lorca's handpuppets poking
their heads out around trees. They're just visiting.
But they could just as easily live here,
making a song and dance of it. All these poets
trying to make sense of presence. Counterweight,
throw of the dice: a gamblers' den.

Spreading boundaries
spreading wings
internal exile stings
parameters: a bracing morning expanding the lungs
beyond inheritance's mining disease.

FENCING REVERSALS

You wouldn't read about it: me putting a fence *in*
rather than taking out; but today, that's just
what I did — I can barely hit the hard green keys
of the priest's old typewriter, fingers so cut,
scratched, pierced and punctured.

But measuring from the western survey peg
with its tomb-markings, and measuring
145 metres up the hill, we restored
the corner post. And that's short of what
they say it should be: think triangularly.

But as the car rally is almost upon us,
every sapling, tree and ant nest (Thurston
asked who lives with ants by choice), enclosure
becomes safer. The stampede is upon us.
Portaloos (blokes won't use) and booze.

I gather in with bloody hands.
Next autumn they'll burn away
from the fence-line. The new one. Ground
gained. Inside I will choke on smoke
and pray the flames away.

Fenced in, the law plays its little defences.
Not the enemy of my enemy, but whatever
stops an enemy getting its claws in,
ignoring the prints of many animals
needing to find their way through red tape.

As the Maun pliers twist wire to wire, rough circuits,
Mick drives past, reverses, plunges down the gravel shoulder
and says, Gidday. We shake hands. A year gone by. This
is temporary, I say, caught in the crosshatched shadows
of loose fencewire. To be strained for restraint. Yeah, he says
after an expectant pause, We'll be off there . . . to England . . . next year —
Trentbridge and Lords test matches. And while you've been over
there, we've pushed a highway of a firebreak all the way
through to Picnic Hill. We don't need to explore issues.
What we each think is already agreed upon if not written.
But he's personable and straight down the line (the loose
fence wobbles). We're out of here for the rally tomorrow,
I say, still at the fence which will hopefully hold *them* out.
Yeah, he muses, enjoying it, we'll have thirty at our place
drinking heaps and watching. Okay, mate, each to his own.
As long as they leave this place alone, cradled in their road
closures. Those fences, all those fences of the loop, the valley:
my collisions, collusions, escapes and imprisonments,
nightmares and dreams of Wallace Stevens, papertigers
squeezing in and out of Jam Tree Gully, welcome and unwelcome,
clear as a bell in the hills, but always suspect, the roar
of worked-over cars. Bloody survey plans: missing pegs,
hidden telephone lines. Wary, wary. Maun pliers twisting
wire to wire, rough circuits as the conversation idles.

FENCING REVERSALS 3

Feel good from labouring. Exhaustion liberates.

Just beyond the front door
a nankeen kestrel lands close
to John and me: it sideswipes
with a glance, hesitates, launches.
Closest I've come to one here.
A gesture of return or coincidence.
Either way. Even a lining up
of planets. End result.

A western gerygone lands on a section of fence
we've just secured. That *ism* between star pickets,
one post to my right, looking nor'west. Working
swings and roundabouts, holding on but not
for grim life, work slower and at a gentler pitch.
But determined. I dare not risk saying the bird
enjoys, but I can say it sticks with it and makes
that characteristic 'plaintive descending call'.

A cohort of '28s'
flies too fast
over the dead parts:
good sense, no doubt,
but giving little hope
to birds that hang around,

whose array of senses
are likely out of synch,
rescue beacons muffled
by ash.

BLANDISHMENTS: 'NI DIEU NI MAÎTRE!'

Sweet compliments to the bigot's ear:
he takes no prisoners, he eats people,
commits atrocities, hears only his own
council. All else is the wishy-washy
compromise of compassion, a tripping
of the circuits, no matter the logic
of allowing the great tree to grow older
or the animal to keep out of range
of metaphoric incisors. Bitter bastards,
he and his apologists. Let me tell you
how sweet it is out here with the percussion
of rifle shots, rally cars roaring past
as we stay locked-down behind pink
warning signs: triangles of the conquest,
as we toss and turn on our own tales
of Hoffmann. Shock feeds its own set
of blandishments. No asset-rich poets
care for the mutual aid of such principles.
But fear the guns, especially at night.
Wealth might ease the warp, the heft,
of Gods, of Masters, and Critics,
through its lavish use of dead colours?
Sweet compliments to the bigot's ear.

Response relies on induction's coils
which are disconnected at the time,
direct current bravado booster
in abeyance, but still, it registered
and simmered without umbrage
or high dudgeon on the behavioural
templates. The Lesson: let them dance
their live band around the bonfires,
plying their trade of ricochet, shots
across the valley: barbed wire
resonance, snare's entanglements.
The stompers and shouters
have a rip-roaring time, revved up
and full of burn-outs, distilled
in their rage their rave their loss.
A parallel circuit: one drops
but the party keeps pumping.
Howz ya therapy goin'? asks
the old establishment bottom-feeder
as you limp bruised through town,
your objections trailing like ignominy.
Believe it or not, this is the same town
in which the wheatbelt anti-misogynist
rape horror film *Shame* was shot
and shot. The hosts sent the message
out via 'social media': 'Come
for bonfire, cars and women!'

THE COONDLE ELEGIES

Bobtail skin — fat and flexibly crisp — shucked
in a roll of fencing wire in the red shed: not dead
the bearer of dead skin, expanded even. Not quite
an elegy of living into habitat reduction. What kind
of contradictory or ecstatic or emphatic elegy
is this? At this precise point, Tracy said a car
from the loop racing the clock would crash
and it did. Through a fence into someone's living.
Perhaps they were okay with risk, celebrating
tension in a portaloo strategically located,
tilting shit downhill. The rubber scriptures,
tyre tithes, jungle-play among small holdings:
grand open market and competitive swipe,
the logos and slogans of the only ones who'd
insure with glee: Shannons. Brand-placement
in the documentary eclipse of the organic.

2.

The hope repetition will make tradition.
Force-fed, battered people who get a taste
for the formula and endless distension
of their orifices: stimulation must be half-
way to something, surely, like street lights
or surveillance cameras. A snapping
telephone. Bite! Bite! When the drought
sweeps back in and the dunnart hangs in
there on surfeit insects unbalanced,
drinking their blood. I will keep

the mental map of where I've seen them
to myself. Selfishness? Stepping cautiously.
I won't call them 'Gilbert's dunnarts',
as they're not and never were, though
he plundered ('collected') them for John
Gould, in whose name I belonged
to the naturalists' club at primary school,
and raised four-hundred dollars to save
birds and tortoises at Blue Gum Swamp.

3.

Young men buy up properties from their one-month
on, one-month off fly-in fly-out gigs on the mines.
They bring greed with them and turn ground inside out,
sucking what they can out of their month's leisure.
It's a good deal for the new world order which they're
part of and embrace so compassion is latitude
the environment won't bear: metaphor is worthless.
Like blank cigarette packets the brand inside still kills.
Sociologists can ride pillion to all of this but we
have to live within the fallout. Pietry (pious poetry)
is funded by ALCOA and BHP. Or the virus
that's got inside, shuffling, switching and rearranging
birdsong so tune and lexicon don't match visuals:
de-speciesisation and re-alignment, the 'best of'
remade in the ultimate hack, all guide books
redundant forever, outside gadgets' stock-taking.

4.

Louche always grabs its place, side-splitting
energy for its affirmation; or sidling furtive
as its calculated smile to take the prize

that we might not even recognise as having worth
but will eventually, when it shines loud
from Louche's snappy pocket. To frolic
in heritage waste, supplant and replant
with nano-blasts of infiltration: their freedom,
their freedom, their choices imposed: ruminate
on that! And if you're following the intertextual
narrative you'll expect some kind of retaliatory
gesture. There is none. The regaining won't happen
by our hands. Not even fingerprints remain.

5.

The half-fallen tree I am preparing to cut up,
saw into parts that will mewl in the firebox,
might be called a 'limb' of the greater tree:
a horizontal rather than vertical take
on growth; I insist we discuss this
in terms of hemispheres and lobes,
of right sides telling left sides
and vice versa; I insist the immolation
of parts is called 'incineration'
rather than warmth, mere warmth.

MOB!

Gentle with that exclamation.
Silent. Now, look through the window:
the mob are nearby, settling in to graze,
five does, two joeys in pouches, and a boomer.
The older rules of co-existence have been evoked,
and the pact back into play. Us mob and their mob,
skirting the edges of day: their 'evening' feed
before retiring under trees for the day
is our 'morning', a little later because
it's not a school day. Thus crossing paths.

You say, Mob! loud in your head, shaking
off sleep (or sleeplessness), and allowing
softest words past your lips: look out
through the blinds, they are here,
all of them. Close by, whispering
among themselves.

CODA

This mob has since been deleted
by good citizens of the neighbourhood.

RETURNS

Where the trees go down
there are no saplings
to fill the gaps.

.

Moss grows
where water
has rolled.

.

Two red-capped robins
just after dawn: two blokes
negotiating territory:

silver-topped rain-
water tank, over-stretched
bough of a hollowed eucalypt. Twins?

.

The sky blue
but the sun nowhere
to be seen.

.

The sun blasting
a cloudless
grey sky.

·

Spring pairing(s)

Black-faced cuckoo shrike
lands on   fence   crosspost
another alights on a wattle
sapling: spring-loaded.

·

I've broken out
of the open sunny places
into the shade & entanglement.

·

Living triangles:
hypotenuse spine
bending right away.

·

Star of David
in the 'tangle':
wattles and York gums:

an eye point
right through
post-blue sunset.

.

Uranium land
(eight hours' drive north)
has its own way

of speaking:
disturb its rest
and it will come back

at the final echo
with strength
of experience.

Don't underestimate
how cold it can get here at night,
around dawn. Minus five
sometimes, often below zero.
That's on clear winter nights.
When it clouds over
the temperature rises.
It doesn't snow
(though it has flurried
unofficially, bringing
denial denial denial).

So when the first bobtail
to allow itself seen as winter
closes and September
days warming
nights still chilly, plays
its ambiguities, we
latch onto portent.

The bobtail emerges
from beneath boulders,
its colouring slightly
off, and much skinnier
than any bobtail
I've previously seen.
Woken too soon
but just in the nick
of time, tail emptied
of hibernation fat.

In cold, patchy sunlight
it is barely articulate.
Sluggish reptile. Unable
to jump-start, catch
its faster prey. It
needs more than slug
sustenance. Hoodwink
of orbit when tilt
is the arbiter.

Don't underestimate
the thermostat
of a famished bobtail:
suddenly brisk
with vulnerability,
snapping its jaws shut
to leave a sore
that will never heal.
Or so it is said.

TRISTIA STORM

A silver storm, a white light storm that ate the sun
and supplanted day-night dialectics, always false in the face of cold
light and trees down (going down as you look) outside, the scribble
of branches across glass that might blow inwards as someone calls your name
from deep inside: John, stand back from the window! as a prayer
crashes to the ground and a confused white-faced heron is a flame

with thunder, and roos gather beneath clumps of York gum, flame-
damaged years back and now clotting at their charred bases, dead sun
in their aspect, forced from one exile into the heart of another no prayer
will lift or drag you out of, none transverse, the unique sharp cold
that isn't analogous to other colds, to snow colds, its name
in recovery, its name a howling and a whisper, or scribble

where creatures under bark mark dead rings. I scribble
my name on official documents, I blow the darkening flame
of the fireplace, thick comportments of wandoo; the name
of the saint who would claim the wood isn't there, absent as the sun
which will break through like pathos and reassurance, its cold
stubble mimesis as raingauge fills with the finishing rain's prayer.

The red storm came with dry breath then furious blood; no prayer
could deflect its onslaught. Today, it's a silver reckoning, scribble
in the margins of holy texts, incidental reading to keep the cold
from a vague idea of 'soul' after all efforts to heat fail, the flame
of the fire pulling in more heat than it could ever give, a sun
in the cold of space: distant, suspicious, questionable, without name.

I am no longer interested in the names of places, things, in the name
of one or many, in the name I might have been given, the prayer
they uttered on my naming day. I was named after a gift, the sun
a gift, and what God does or says or gives away is scribble
on our DNA, as the flipside of wattle-leaves glowers silver flame
as cold as lies as cold as truth as cold as legacy as *cold cold cold*.

It's not yet safe to venture outside to survey to embrace the cold
residue of conflict, afflictions of faith, difficulty in attaching name
to the central thesis of self, the fate of the young echidna whose flame
burns bright on a dark day, its diurnal caution shucked off: no prayer
will keep it safe in failure to read storm codings, its brazen scribble
of quills staggering through granites, termiteground soft for digging sun.

The opening out of cold vistas where storm has smashed aside with prayer
or despite prayer, where no name will halt the rewriting of place, no
    scribble
enact or destroy leafage and bough, no flame rejuvenate what burnt hot as
    the sun.

I MISTAKE THE SCENE(RY)
FOR A PAINTING

Window frame. Reflection off glass.
Angle of perception. But mainly clear
images. Storms that stripped leaves away
relish the house now visible across the valley.
How does the artist suggest this in one frame?

I can hear (and identify) birds but can't see any.
Two separate processes. Looking at the painting
of the window, and hearing the real world
behind it. Or auditory hallucination, positing
which birds would be there if the artist has been
sensitive or without agenda. A wind blows but leaves are still.

But then, heavy-set trunks seem fragile (I know termites
have hollowed away, that bees, reptiles and birds nest
in there), and sway despite the leaves' stolid resolution.
The deception of colour, wattles lamp-lighting to suggest
where sun comes from, those little tricks of lighting.

And I can see the pencil (HB) sketch beneath the oil's
thick and thin application. Maybe the smoothing of canvas
warp: texture you might fall into, smashing the glass,
fatally wounded. The red beneath the truth of those siennas
and ochres, stark black fenceposts to orientate by. Perspective.
Clouds pitch on their rolling wave of blue and grey, sway.

There are no animals at all. No, flashes of black and white,
'tabby', wild cats flashing past, one up a tree, swaying. But
all is still — that's not possible. Mind playing tricks.
Eyesight deteriorating further. Overactive imagination.
Tendency to repetition. How else to interpret signs of painting?

THE PAINFULLY RED OBJECT
ACROSS THE VALLEY

A hideous penetrating red you won't find in 'nature'.
Synthesised red on the edge of the bush, declarative
on the jaw of valley. A violent red pulled molar.

Were it just, say, scarlet and obnoxious because of this
I wouldn't make a song and dance, but it's dead red. Odious
mono-technicolour raincoat, sapped of all but horrors of red.

No need to list different grades of red for effect.
Each spectrum adjustment a musical outcome. The painfully
red object across the valley is a trick, an entry in the book

of extinction, a parody of warning, an absorber of colourful
parrots; the qualities of red distract from the certainty
of its calling. Operating machinery you'll be corner-eyed,

caught out, cut short, sliced to the quick, spilling life- blood
onto old soil. Red is as red does. It makes nature. It en-natures
the valley's ashen floor, its cuboid intensity a tomb-marker

for ancient flooded gums with incinerated hearts.

FERAL TOMCAT'S TERRITORIAL GAINS

That muscle-bound compact feral tomcat
riding roughshod over conviction and addiction
to faith, lifelonging or lifeforce of all else
in its territory, within talon-range.
Kick-arse, muscles toned with a stretch.
The politics of calling out: brutal, ruthless,
deadly: who would stand in its way
should it come into range, hellbent?
All cat angst and envy, all self-hypnotism
and glands. The sky it stalks beneath
a mirror. It's a beauty, exemplar adaptation
and application shuffling evolution
along a dodgy track. Why
blood boils in our veins
(a fever that comes and goes),
wearing its influence, stalking
and watching us, carefully, hesitating
to look over shoulder before bolting.
Not being carnivorous doesn't mean
I neglect totting up its victims: rare and common species,
native and introduced: though wondering
why cityfolk making weekender tree-changes
drag their placid kitties up to let them experience
the great outdoors, buttering their paws,
bemused when lovely birdies vanish.
Pulchritude and the boss tomcat: beauty in the eye,

thrillkill. Bush *will* submit. Tomcat
might eat offspring in the monstering
excitement: all that transplanted
and reconfigured beauty, the ugliness
of plastic surgery.

GATHERING KINDLING WITH TIM
WHILE THE SEASONS CHANGE
SLIGHTLY AS WE WALK

It's getting warmer and the fire is lit late in the day,
just before the sun sets on the hills and the distant coast
hangs to its longer light. I take Tim out to help collect
kindling to feed the next few days burnings. Snakes
are just starting to wake after disturbed and uneasy
winter sleep, unsure which season they are rising
to, unsure of the messages of their blood, the weather.
I warn Tim to be wary and watch carefully where he treads.

Tim is distracted by ants. He is compiling a book
of the many species of ants at Jam Tree Gully. He notes
that he has not been able to study their movements,
their homes, their empires, for over a year. He considers
himself an authority on what can be seen by the observer
who doesn't intrude, doesn't get in the ants' way.
This is probably true. He studies black ants, sugar ants,
red ants, green ants, bull ants and other more esoteric
species. Collecting kindling he also watches for ants.
It's a plot to go where he can't go unaccompanied.
That's okay. He's mapping and remapping. If there's
a colonialism of mapping he is reinventing the notion
of 'map'. He makes lists. He copies logos. He remembers
words, their pronunciations, their meanings. He translates.

It's getting warmer and the fire is lit late in the day,
just before the sun sets on the hills and the distant coast
hangs to its longer light. Tim is working on his Ants Book,
and looks up and mentions that the fire's taken hold

in the firebox: 'some of that kindling was collected
by me.' We both know it has been checked thoroughly
for ants at the moment of collection, and that ants
hold sway. As the growing warmth breaks down cold
over coming weeks, the ants will gain true dominion.
From skerricks of moisture in faucets, traces of stickiness
on table or benchtop, crumbs spilt on the floor, especially
beneath Tim's seat. Tim is distracted by ants. The room is warm.

CARNABY'S COCKATOOS AT NEW NORCIA

The Moore or Maura River flows
steadily and filmically over the ford;
in twisted roots of melaleuca
working green water with its platelets
and clots of algae broken up in quasi-rapids,
the conflicted smoothness of roots that ghost
and trap human imagination before the dry
empties the river, takes moisture deep below
the bed, pools quivering with heatwaves;
there a rat stirs against daylight, and the shimmer
of water bifurcating and recollecting,
flycatchers frantic where water appears
to slow — delusion — and insects skitter
up and out; to sketch this as a blur
of interdependent colour, to skip outlines
or signs of echo in water feeding out
(a gilgie aerating?), twists music
to silence, a monastic bell
ringing time from its tower,
and Carnaby's cockatoos traumatised
by a lack of nesting sites, lack of familiar
aerial photographs, drop flocks to three or four
and break out where there is less familiar land,
another name to be strung onto, songs
lampooning their own productions
(stereos in utes fitted with spotties,
stereos syncopating the rough and the smooth),
where a road once cut through from monastery
to Wyening, outpost forty kilometres away
and now a track of dead-ends, though water

still flows when it falls away, and the coast
calls inland inland, wanting all liquid
even lead melted for slugs left in cockatoos.
Just sketch the river, the tormented roots
of paperbarks, gnarled bolls of flooded gums
with their outbursts, insects working hard
amidst the nitrogenous, the oily, the Maura.

CANOLA ANTI-PRAYER (NEW NORCIA 2)

Our prayers are outside
the church; they are sceptical
of the burgeoning canola but not the spark
inside and without the living plant.
Whatever is done, yellow
sacraments host elements
of scoured and poisoned soil
that ants lift against tribulation,
each flower a light each flower
a prayer for seed that might
perpetuate without commerce.

Our prayers are outside
the church; in the star, gravity,
craven yellow dark, stretched
light. All that is canola.

Our prayers are outside
the church; you can't help
the uplift, even with hay-fever
burying you: prayers outside
this field of vision, though litany,
chants and recitation seep through stone
piled against harsh weather, cool
when sun burns bright either side
of shade, designed to elevate
the field of yellow flowers
it is set against. No *son et lumière.*

BROTHER (NEW NORCIA 3)

Searching for his crowd
out of the silence of the cloister,
black robes tousled by the nor'-wester,
first bite of heat caught on the brim
of his wide, black hat. Tim says,
'Were you in there, Mum?' 'No, I was
in one for women, Tim, and it wasn't
the same architecturally, though
there are some similarities.'
'Were you a nun, Mum?'
'I was training to be a nun,
but I left and had you instead,
and I am very glad I did.'
Blessed. We will photograph
and sketch and write the river,
the swollen flooded gums,
the yellow crops. The brother,
passing, smiles and nods
in acknowledgement of Tracy's 'Hello'.
I get it. I do. And we come here
with something half in mind: polar
opposites yet not cancelling
or missing out. But not balancing
either: we have seen storms brew
over old buildings here, and know
histories of conquest, the prayers
they take to put into effect,
the weight of habit and spiritual

cleanliness. Yet for all that,
we come back, and fluttering robes
are the night and the day,
the body of one, the one body.

FOXES STRUNG UP ON FENCE ON
TOODYAY-BINDI BINDI ROAD:
IN THE ACCUSATIVE

On land cleared to a few trees
you say you're protecting
native wildlife (but not kangaroos,
because 'they're feral by any
other definition'); you tell us
that you're a safe user
of firearms, protecting lambs
you'll send to slaughter;
you string foxes up on fences
so the public can know
what it's like to fight for a cause,
corpses of enemies piled high
for the townsfolk to file past
and know the cost of battle.
The cost of the kill,
pride in marksmanship,
celebration and mateship.
Your triumphs are the triumphs
of ancient Rome, of death squads
anywhere anytime; such a timeless
occupation. Good thing there's
no bounty on animal libbers
and greenies, as you might just
be tempted to break the rule
of robotics not to kill humans;
for the general good, the cause.
Foxes strung out on a fence
show us you'll stand up and be counted,

O mighty warriors of the farmlands.
We've known your spotlights
probe into our houses at night.
We live with that. We catch our breath
and watch our words. The dead fox.
The dead cat. The dead roo.
The dead the dead the dead.

GHOST TROPHIES

The ghosts of a dozen
executed foxes, strung up
along a fence on
the Toodyay-Bindi Bindi Road
latched on to a passing car
in broad daylight
and pleaded for release,
for the grace of burial,
for the trophy of light
in dark eyes.

Blurred in their
manifestations, though
precise as decay
on pinched strands
of prick-wire, thonged
to sky and the wistful
float of rainless clouds;
par-green crops begging
closure, a vista implosion
to snout the ground,
a car's exhaust.

It's the blur
I am writing off.
Corpses, their ghosts,
their need to attach
is second nature.
Here. Hear. Here.

BUSH THANATOS

Paint a colourfield
of furs or pieces to shorten
the life of canvas;

hangdog look
moon on tips of needles:
quills

pray or curse by,
rouse up old gods to find
'file not found';

call of the wild
versus
'call of the wild';

kudos
service
apogaeum;

love urge
to decorate
semi-nuptial beds;

skite bounty unto
vixen and kits, make heart
of sleeve;

bloody bush of tail
though blood runs to snout
with hanging.

FRANKENTHALER AT JAM TREE GULLY: (NO) *MOUNTAINS AND* (NO) *SEA* (1952)

Mountains and sea are a long way from here.
One mountain is within driving range,
but the nearest chain is far south and eroded.
We are on the edge of hills, shoulder
of a range that reaches down to the plains.
Sea is a flavour of breeze or the kick
of a winter storm fed by valleys
far away. Colour seeps back and forth:
'landscape in my arms as I did it':
mottles up awash to particularise
                        circuit of states: gaseous act of seeing,
fluid exhibition, inhabitation of what's gone back over

remember seeing: colour is fingerprint
                greenly piquant (leaf litter)
        archaic uses of egregious
sets the polluted river on its estuarial watch
to suit development collocations (yes, 'heinous crime' IS
apt)
        all that's left intact is the act
of seeing, splashing in the rock, climbing faces
of waves;

                but sea wrestles with horizontals, a curve
complex, calenture betrayed by swell
and dead coral underpinnings:
                                'mass,' says the critic
'eats at edges of heartland, as patriotic subterfuge';

consequent sails plume to clam the resistant
to occupy in studio aftermath

                              concomitant to gnash
against the rocks and wash up wheatbeach
burials: shared history, shared gestations
of charrings.

MAUVE DISTRICT
(FRANKENTHALER, 1966): 2012

Sunset and this is it. This is that.
I'd fill it with Nude, but it doesn't
look the part. Nude is more or less,
and moves differently. Each her own.
Each face each sun each opacity on the window.
It's a precise map here where maps are doubtful.

I'd swear more it's the southwest shape
I'd swear the shape midpoint of hillside
looking out I'd swear the mauve is shape
I am inside looking out into, I'd swear.

Yes, yes, edges and light here, too.
But no luck in the degraded off-green
which hangs in there: scraped, dug, weeded
out to meet shire quotas to fuel unloading
continuous occupation in bundles of lingering
daylight to placate night's desire for absolution.

I left off this image because the light wasn't right:
not nearly mauve enough which bespoke qualities
elicited from even thin-lensed eyesight searching
for colour to sign off, relocate certainty in shadow
or trees obscuring starlight, but less than warmth
was never mauve enough: Now, it is right. Now!

I'd swear more it's the southwest shape
sold as visit to this state of solid light,
place of transition and leisure where locals
wear costs without complaint: dipping with sunlight.

UNCANNY RURAL, SEXUAL POLITICS AND FRANKENTHALER'S *NATURE ABHORS A VACUUM*

Roaming outside in the fullness of grass, dirt, fences,
trees, animals and insects, plethora of birds, poison on the air
and sweet nectars, grizzly pollens and wasp galls felling
wattles, in the fullness of fire-risk to come the red
conflagration on the edge of mind or sudden and full
of fear and caution driving some to reveal themselves
to rudiments of nature, building-blocks of elements,
stark on their hills, not a leaf to combust not an insect
to flutter though termites move underground towards
plant fibre, soaked to kill to ward off even the possibility,
as large as sky as disruption in atmospheric certainty,
abhorring all nature and sucking the little clear air
into the vacuum of their lungs' life-spans, but still grim
at grey horizon (sharp, delineated), and thankful
yet ready to spread messages when flukes and colorations
of disaster strike elsewhere, houses so exposed carried off
by freak gusts before differentiating howls past, present, future
occupations of space they count as theirs, small flat
gardens relying on too much water, exotic pot plants
swinging on verandahs battling for shade, the harsh sun
and awkward sky. And elsewhere, traces of blood
rolling off resistant soils, spoiling their patch.

CATERPILLAR TIME

and (partially) thinking of Frankenthaler's
Yellow Caterpillar (1961)

One sections its way along the wall at right angles to round
the square off, hypotenuse its convertible self.

Bursting with transformative zeal and information, it homes
in on a place of purchase.

Shuffle leg diorama shunting appendages on scruffy bark
to reach lush leaf fans.

Yellow interior is not digestive hoodwink but internal aura
I can only guess at — all external beauty, holy inside & out.

Head reaching up to blue slab of sky and knitting vista
with immaculate movements of mouth,

never allow accidents when they cross the paths: never never never:
keep an eye out as they do, close to it all. Real close.

Soft sparks to jump gaps everywhere out there: or suckering
up the window to reveal the belly of the future.

We are talking about art here. Just because I look out into
a caterpillar world of Latin names and their backwash . . .

Between stages maybe, but such glorious intactness and self-
sufficiency. Glory glory glory.

Conversions of moisture and dryness, solidity and fluidity
in the crossing and dwelling. The hairiness.

Dark markers of digested presence to give back and sign,
never retaliate though some parody the fierce.

At the precise point of day when last rites are taken: the day
predator birds last gasp last swoop heat signature switching over

to nightbirds infra red standover tactics but to be pierced
to the vitals by the last swoop of day murdered

as dark falls, nightcap where weird isn't a word with grip
as the gatekeepers condemn analogies.

HINT FROM FRANKENTHALER

(after *Hint from Bassano*, 1973)

Craven as flight, unremitting
as eye clashing with ear,
stumbling towards Egypt,
the entire family loaded
with an angel winging
a path of light: discordant
and smooth, precise as wind
rippling over grass (inside of a wave)
outside your window as if beauty is in every
grain of sand lodging in cracks,
gritting up the works.

When green and blue are no longer here, exile is beyond redemption.
Angles of disquietude containing smudge of lifespan and mechanism
of movement, tamas and hope as burning aftermath: chill effect
in the heat, land's backwash an injection of your own blood
into the failure of colour, labile saturate loss, though impelled
forward as back isn't an option and sideways disperses manifests
and records journeys, how much is in the stroke of chronicle,
or wing strokes and the uplift playing off the muted downforce.

                          Degeneracy of green, spread
                          sheet to catch fallout, driven
                          servitude and mastery, granaries
                          of GM corn enveloped from imposed

rat tumours, exceeding the 90 days
test limit though still denied
by the village's scribes and despots
and their patrician rushes of blood.

TESTIMONIAL

Wattle yellows the valley.
Repetition is *lazy*
though I have back-aches
and blisters.
Work outside
is not work on the page.
Betwixt dirt and paper
the risk of conjunctions.
Of mistaking the measure:
quotidian, prosaic,
concomitant.

'INCURSION' OF NATIVE
BLUE-BANDED BEES

As if domicile and houseplans
can ward off or refute the rarity
of the native blue-banded bee
at this butt end of the Darling Ranges.

As if the word 'incursion' might
prevent owning up to flightpaths
and stimulus of heat to burrow
and nest: vents in windows

to prevent winter condensation
open to the searching urge
of the blue-banded now their
time has come (the European

honeybees are plethoric
in the gully below, filling
the hollowed York gum by the sluice
a storm cut a month or so ago).

Head in and back out, reverse
park, no space for manoeuvre,
securing a false drill-hole in an eave.
Some window-vents less ideal

than others, open straight into the cool
expanse of the human house,
no comforting 'claustrophobia',
but a dimensional shift in evolution.

As intense a buzz as any 'introduced'
honey-makers' fate to profit by,
swinging into belonging
on the besieged block,

in and on the 'our'. Remark the metallic
blue bands of a less damaging
evolution: technology sharp
as light and procreation.

CONFUSION OF THE SENSES

After fifteen days driving the continent
and two days of intense grass cutting, there is a sludge
in my mucous membranes and my senses are overloaded.
It's been a hot day and wild oats higher than myself
are still green at the base, tangling and knotting the head
of the whipper-snipper. Blue butterflies lift from the cut,
the tattered haloes of fallen grass. The sun is making
its evening spectrum on hills across the valley,
and no colour I recognise or would risk naming
is on display. It's truly *otherworldly*, even repellent.
I am out of alignment and disturbed: the cutting,
the thickness of hands (my brother, a shearer,
lives with this), the many cuts from stones flung hard.
Into the red shed to pour fuel Tracy has collected
and mixed for the two-stroke, I am floored by a stench:
something dead? In failing light I scout around the great
barren cathedral, and see nothing, though wonder
if some rodent or reptile or even small marsupial
has buried itself under the pallets of hay still left
from when the shed was a stable, its incarnation
in the time of a previous owner; or if a creature
has tunnelled into the dross of the horse stall,
spacious and otherworldly in itself, a section
into which I never set foot. I detect some diggings
at its centre but no trails in-out. The stench is absolute —
I can't source or follow it anywhere in particular.
It is anomalous in the wastes of the building,
not a place I often visit, a place with its own reality.
I step outside and survey the grass still to be cut,
the stench reaching out faster than I can close the door.

The storm is giving us a good bashing.
A pummelling. Work with it as the pings
take out car and butterflies not making
the verandah are sadly (catastrophically)
shredded. It's brutal.
                          Ear-bashing, side-splitting,
tub-thumping, snare, kettle, bass and tophat.
Entertainment of apprehension.
What's to clean up, crashing
the rain-gauge, waiting for heat to melt
hail to make measurement.
                          Curious the synthesis
disruption makes to status quo: mosquitoes
appear spontaneously, rare birds put on a post-
event show, and a new orthography
sets to work indoors: notch up another
to survival, the verandah clinging on
despite shadecloth prised away,
going going gone.
                    And of the hail itself:
imperfect, lopsided and inconclusive
for all its wallop. Putting the mockers
on a critical day: severe fire warning,
all work called to a halt: a peppering
of the just and unjust alike, a quip. Opaque.
Not at all glasslike.
                    The bruised stubble

smells bitter and taunted: bread half-baked, smoke
without flame though lightning forks
across the valley, almost striking
those dry, grassed hills.

MUMMIFIED FROG

Set to leap as heat rises
and moisture fails; to huddle
down to a nervous crouch,
fading colours, contracted skin,
eyes routed and bones
locked into place,
no longer camouflage
then camouflage grey
parchment at the burning
time of year. Still out there,
on yellow sand, intent,
so dry and complete
not even ants bother it;
transformation, embodiment
of afterlife, decay
stopped dead
in its tracks.

Witnessing night and day
with equal veracity,
quality of membrane
no nostalgia to be held up
to those who live
and breathe in the vicinity.
There's no wish to drag down,
to make others pay.

But tension to leap
endures, encased as stone.
Active on an atomic level

or smaller, holding in
the chain reaction
which might be rage
in a *lesser* creature,
or belief that it lives.

BROWN FALCON

Brown falcon profits from the cut grass
and all stirred up: the grey burrows of grasses
woven as wombs, empty now as the roar and whine
of the cutter approaches, and seasonally so,
and all that moves ahead of the onslaught.

Brown falcon perches on the lowest branch
of an acacia just beyond the window: one eye
on me, one on the ground not far below. Its drop
is no plunge, and like a skydiver or base jumper
with too little air left to open a chute, it tumbles
onto its target. I know not what it caught,
if anything at all. I look away. Complicit.

Back on its low perch vertex
the brown falcon puts horror
into the hearts of songbirds
in the silver-green swathe
of jam tree above. It hunts
or pauses below, I don't know,
but if it strikes it will
strike upwards, or make
a mental note, a brain map,
fly down and out, up and over
and drop down into foliage
from a vantage of impaired
vision, muted line of sight
knowing what's what
and where's where
from its time below.

RESTORATIVE

'kind of catchy'
SYD BARRETT

With wild oats ten-foot high where water
wells in granite fonts, where roots are baptised
and reborn to say, 'We're genetically okay here,
we're a super strain that'll drink the plenty
despite bleak red rebarbative dirt closing in,
that'll choke an airfilter when disturbed,
gather on lungs to kill you off later, just as skin
cancers accrue because the sun's bite
is everything dominant, and not a scheme
of rhyme or reason swollen with false memory,
the odour of tap water on hot bricks — an urban
myth or true encounter? — the convulsions
of olfactory parochialism.' What to do with
this later in life? I tell you, I ache all over,
barely able to note down the statistics
of a day's labour, separate off what was learnt
from wild oats today or much, much earlier.

TWO BOATS ON THE FIREBREAK

for Alfred Wallis's *Two Boats* (circa 1928)

Two redbrown boats with redbrown sails
lit up my air the grey, bare board of earth
(landfall, slurry at the bottom of an old sea), lit up
on the firebreak curving down gully and capillaries
flecked with yellow silage, adrift the chaffed
grassland intrusions and interpolations,
two redbrown boats on a redbrown firebreak
with yellowing white caps, sliding downhill,
single mast and three sails, mainsail confidence
and jib sail sparing with squalls to bite ends off
life pattern unfurling tugging ropes to leeward
curving profile I see dip below lower canopies,
the angles we perch on and see by, landfall at hand,
so near, so near and so far and so treacherous
where mapped most, where sailed most frequently.
Gone — dipped below horizon of redbrown firebreak.

SKITTISH

Post- the shoot-'em-up, a joey is skittish
on the firebreak. I go to check, to see
if there are injuries. Sentinel boomers
have gone. Not hard to guess. Two does
and two joeys, all that's left of the mob,
burying themselves in the reserve's
long wild oats, in the place where
the shire will burn through next autumn
to diminish or delete the little shelter left.
Back in the firing line, slightly older,
wondering what instinct means
and what should be added
to the list, the tab.

THIS IS NO STOCKADE

This is no stockade
to keep them out;
this is no stockade
to take the brunt;
this is no stockade
to hold its own;
this is no stockade
to flag its moment.
This is no stockade
to vanguard a mine;
this is no stockade
to placate the boss.
This is no stockade
to count our loss;
this is no stockade
to surround or rally 'round;
this is no stockade
to watch over frontiers;
this is no stockade
to make last stands;
this is no stockade
to retreat into;
this is no stockade
from which to rally forth.
This is no stockade
of ordnance or survey;
this is no stockade
to store your relics.

JUVENILE KESTREL, JUVENILE HUMAN

The walk to the boulders is a clear run
now the oats are down, though jags and chunks
of granite, wind-whittled spikes of upturned roots,
the odd abandoned burrow, make this almost a lie.
Yet it looks straightforward enough and the cool
of late afternoon through distended shadows
of wattles and eucalypts means snake-risk
is relatively low, but still an immediate
and present danger. So I take Tim
up to the boulders after school —
he's been at me to let him back up there —
and we make it without incident. He peers
under the ledge of the great boulder
and says, rightfully, it's a strong portal.
Centre of the Earth stuff if you're echidna-sized
and can squeeze through to the expanse beneath.
I keep an eye out for mulga snakes. *One bite*
and all that. But as he investigates and speaks
his own language of boulders and snakes,
I hear a juvenile kestrel and catch it flying past,
lightning-fast against a stark, clear sky,
and rest easy about snakes: such a small bird of prey
could tackle a creature so much larger than itself
and come off best. There's no lesson in this.
No analogy. No fable. And the boy and the kestrel,
though aware of each other and interested,
have their own means and own purposes.
Separated, if connected. Not remotely the same.

A SHORT NARRATIVE OF WILD BEES
AND A TORN CALF MUSCLE

Back-tracking echidna scratchings, curious
as to its place of bunking down, I move close
to a wild beehive in the trunk of the largest
York gum on the block: it is near a crevice
of granite littered with dead wood, a good shelter
for an echidna. In a kind of slow motion up-close horror,
I am stung through my shirt on the shoulder again and again.
I lurch around the rocks, bees swarming in my hair,
grotesque, outlandish, heteromorphically
and preternaturally weird. But not comical. Distance
warps the picture. Humour's little injections of poison:
melittin and histamine. Some need epinephrine,
but I only hurt and swell, though rationale is lost
as well: turning heel, bees at my ankles, I scale
the hill and something tears inside my calf muscle.
I hobble, flailing, infuriating the bees further.
I stagger, shaking them off, slapstick, rising
out of the great tree's opinionated shade
into sunlight. Then everything is flat, dead-
pan. Abandoned on the hillside. The narrative
is Buster Keaton. Or the narrative is passage,
exploration, revelation and escape. I limp home.
The stories I might tell. It grows more dramatic
by the second. The stuff of family myth.
But bees perish in their stinging,
and as I lick my wounds the storylines
break down, just fragments poking through
all those weeks of recovery to look forward to.
So much or too much denouement in the skit.

FERAL TOMCAT'S PISS

Out of the glaring he struts alone
and marks territory with bursts
of pungent piss that mimics or raises
the dead. The red shed with hay
and rodents is his domain,
coming in from the bush
where he answers to no-one
and cuts down all in its path.
He knows ego and uses it: weapon
against domesticated adventurers
whose 'owners' like their vistas
empty and reined in: cats
extensions of foreign policy.

Out of the glaring he struts alone
and marks territory with bursts
of pungent piss that mimics or raises
the dead. He nails his queen
with a caterwaul in the fragile light
of an eroding moon, a breeding
compunction working in conjunction
with a grand plan: progeny
equals inheritance. But he will remain
master of all he sprays until
the last drop of stink, revelling
in his messages, fur and feathers
of the deceased, his fetishes.

THE PARROT POISONERS

The closer they are to death, the more
people want to kill off the beautiful
parrots, the more gardens
and crops seem vulnerable.

The young men score their charts
with fresh kills. Rebelling,
they comply. Youth wants
feeding.

Parrots eat the seed which appears
no less poisoned than what people
harvest to eat themselves.
Looks like good feed.
Parrots young and old
chew with glee.

Colourful corpses will dull
after suffering.
Gone to drop off the perch.
Old men with histories
try not to gloat, old women
say a pest is a pest.

Kids would rather shoot
mid-air at a great distance.
Dead-eyed dicks. But poison
is fascinating and reaches
out over generations,
like a religious feast.

The closer to death the more
they want to kill off the beautiful;
the young score their charts
with fresh kills.

BUSHFIRE APPROACHING

(i)

I am ready to evacuate if need be.
My wife emailed to say a fire is out of control
on Julimar Road, less than ten kilometres away.
She says she'll return with the car, but I say it's okay,
we'll monitor and speak through the gaps.
She insists she will return: listening to the chat
in the library at Toodyay, seeing smoke in the west,
checking the FESA site. I say I will take a look outside
and get back to her in minutes. She is waiting. I climb
the block gingerly with my torn calf muscle striking back,
and see the growing pall over Julimar. A great firebreak
and a bitumen road are between here and there, I reassure,
though I will keep a close eye on it. The breeze blows
from the east, but is ambivalent and could swing
about. There are no semantics in this. And Paul Auster
is right where William (the lumberman) Bronk was wrong:
the poem doesn't happen in words, but 'between seeing
the thing and making it into a word'. *Location location location.*
As evidence: if fire sweeps through, only the mangled
metal of this Hermes typewriter will remain,
a witness, philosophy in-situ vanquished, and an elegy
made from bits of a different seeing with different words,
remain. Figurative density will take hold, and landscape
will be less fragile, the font more robust. It won't rely
on paper: ash become an idea, a taste for some.
You stop seeing the red when it's on top of you.
But true burning feeds on ash and the idea

of fire: it perseveres and requires only oxygen
and memory. Wild oats caught in my socks
taunt my ankles. Fuel for fire. In all seriousness.

(ii)

I am not hearing AC/DC's 'This House is on Fire'
out of perversity. This morning a rush of colour
brought on a flashback, and I've not had one of those
for a decade. Strychnine-saturated, like the bush
where rangers claim to conserve native species
through poisoned baits. Rapid heartbeat, dry mouth,
outbreaks of laughter (grotesque, face of death),
colour codings of annihilation: spiritual and topographical.
Phantasm of acid trips — pink batts, supermen, green dragons,
orange barrels, purple hearts, clearlights, ceramic squares,
goldflakes, microdots, lightning bolts: nomenclature
of William Blake and weird melancholy of habitat loss.
Lost and unfounded. A run on images. Voices in the room.
Excruciating paranoid cartoon violence. So, I check
outside again and the plume is still moving southwest
though the wind is tentative and temperature
up five degrees over the last thirty minutes. This is realtime,
unlike hypnogogia, hallucinations? Grounds for worship.
Foundational ontology. I should mention that I have flu
and that's why I stayed home in the first place. Harvest
is full-on though I have finished grass cutting here.
I wore myself out and my defences are down. Run down.
Antibodies hesitant if not docile. I make rhetoric
out of the flood of image-fragments: seems like good sense,
making the best, keeping a grip, cool in a volatile situation?

(iii)

I'm abandoning my poem on the wheatbelt stone gecko
and the 'keeled tail' of a black-headed monitor
which is running amok through the roof, along walls,
scaling trees with maritime skill. The images lack
explanation and coalesce, are minimalist, but will
serve as a poor kind of last will and testament.
One sheet in my pocket, and it will be this.

(iv)

The wind has dropped, though smoke — not impenetrable
but more substantial than 'thin' — hangs over the block,
a tentative fallout. The birds are doing their silence
thing, or have shot through. We keep no birds in coops.
The air is almost acrid. Defend or abandon?
It's when the smell of burning reaches upwind
that you know it has bitten deep. Firebreaks: check.
Water: check, but if the pump goes that's an end to flow.
Fireblanket: check. Personal papers and evacuation pack: check.
No room for 'literature': just this poem, paperweight.
Ready to lend a helping hand: always, to best of ability.
Essential medications. Maybe the boy's most precious toy,
but he wouldn't expect it. Something of my wife's.
Insects thick on the flyscreens: suddenly Hitchcockian.

(v)

Smoke-mushrooms are haloes about wattles they haven't yet touched
where it counts. Prelude. Early life of devastation, its long legacy
too long in its brief moment of, well, beauty. Back again after
staggering uphill — glimpses of lush green moss amidst stubble
and granite are bemusing and bizarrely cheering — and all is suddenly

military, warzone, combat. Helitacs, fixed-winged water bombers
coming over the hills. Dousing. Or maybe it's anti-militaristic?
No time to think about this. Three years ago, fire destroyed
forty homes just south of here. It was like this then, too.

(vi)

Alert Level: 'a bushfire is burning near Julimar and Kane Roads';
'stay alert and monitor your surroundings'; why use quote marks?
This is barely copyright in the life and death of it. Plagiarism?
Blame burns with a heat unlike any other and burns long
after last embers have faded. And with days of heat and high
winds ahead, even a dead ember might find heart again, and leap
to the occasion. Elemental showdown. Proof. Precedent.
Test case. Habeas corpus — the body present. The burning
question: people build houses in the bush, then blame the bush.
My brother, life-long surfer, says: If I get taken by a shark
remember it was while doing something I love in *its* universe.
Remember me in this light. The fire has jumped Julimar Road.

ARC

An inch of rain in less than an hour
and hillside dissolving
into valley, torn to the quick,
bones broken and swept away,
Toodyay stone bobbing like cork
on instant rapids, to head out
together under the eaves,
ground wet beneath rubber soles,
and as I am about to say, 'Let's keep apart
lest lightning strike one of us
and we arc, leaving Tim parentless,'
the time-rending slash of light,
magnesium-ribbon flare
that blinds in distending
sight into the infinite's
finitude, a slicing apart
of tissue and time, temporal
glitch where thunder and lightning
are one, no counting down to safety,
as just metres away (imperial
and metric anneal), charged steel
fencepost, groundstar telescoped
to firmament, glistens and crackles.
This is as near as Tracy has come
to being struck, heart too fast
then overcome by sleepiness,
taste of sulphur on the tongue;
though I've been here before,
and closer, closer: always
bringing a wry smile

to a listener's lips,
while in mine a twitch
I can't control, calling me
whenever conditions are right.

TARPING THE STACKS

I.

Polyethylene blue reflects a tempestuous sky
with its half-formed features, its blurred vision,
        wishful thinking firmament parody,
        as first fat droplets pit the conical pile
and triangular prism with bevelled edges in the open
        steel-sided bin, reinforced with props
        as you struggle to draw tarps over
volume (thousands and thousands of bushels), wind
        sneaking under followed by violent lift,
        tattered sail, breaking cardinal
rules of safety and form, co-polymer polypropylene
        ropes groaning in grommets, swollen
        lymph nodes. Great bunker covers,
stretched skin over stockpiles of tiny organs, golden
        loot you might surf, a transmogrified
        wave-wall. This is disturbance
of memory as you see men perched precariously,
        after fresh grain is poured in from
        farms after the rough storm, field-
bins drained, but weather's eye still brooding,
        threatening. This is you as a youth,
        grain in your pockets, cuffs, and socks,
even pouched in underwear, taunting genitals;
        a bready poisonous paradox, as steel-
        capped boots sit on asphalt, abandoned,
safety an impractical order of the day: grain
        works and is worked better without
        them; even the bullying among workers

stops — the name-calling, the taunts, the tricks
       verging on negligence — as not working
       together means you'll all be dragged
over the coals for failure, and *coals* in fire season
       are an irreconcilable contradiction.
       To slip might mean a spill, a ride,
a compulsive rush to accident or death,
       knowing that whatever grain
       survives you will be gathered,
stockpiled again, saved: to be sent on to foreign
       and local markets, to be eaten
       in any corner of the earth
to stave off famine, taken for granted,
or whipped into indulgent luxury food items.

2.

From here, a fair distance away, the man on top
of the stack, controlling the 'rapid deployment' of tarp,
       its unfurling towards the end of the bin's
       baking tin, is all fingers and thumbs:
we might see his overlong nails, caked with grain dust,
       gripping at the heavy-duty blue tarp,
       too thick for nails to tear or puncture,
no matter how hard he grips, wrestles sail to the wind
       which is much stronger up there. In his
       struggle, all his enmities are expressed:
but we can't pin this on him, though you can make
       out a grimace that is more than risk
       or physical pain, what's kept in or out.
Another bloke joins him aloft; they work against each other
       before finding the grain of the grain
       and moving with it: whatever slips

aside, whatever gathers in streams and avalanches
        incidental to the horizons which falls
        away at the rims, a curving call,
never steady on your feet but going with it,
        sea-legs deep in wheatlands. Tarp
        overlaps tarp, knitted and cross-lashed,
bound-down taut surface to slide down, child-
        like, gleaming tension held snugly
        over underworld of seed and dust
grown in the bones and stories of clearing. Down
on the ground, shaky and unable to walk the line.

SCARECROWS

No real need for scarecrows around here:
most of the grain-inclined birds are killed
and the few left don't scare easily
or have seen it all and more. Still,
some newer farmers give it a go: jackets
flapping in the breeze, troubled grins, eyes
that see far beyond their fate; but more aesthetics
than end results. And some old-timers
rustle up wooden crosses and coat hangers
in their fields, distressed figures
troubled by colourful parrots
nibbling at their responsibilities.
But few, very few. Shotguns
in the pantry.

GATHERING EVIDENCE

Tracking through the reserve at 5pm through 5.40pm.

Young guy in white four-by-four with dual spotties
On the roof crossbar was cruising past above our block
Again: watching, studying. On Saturday I saw him
Emerge from the reserve over our crossover
Onto the Loop. He went past twice earlier today.
I know what watchers do — I have come across
This precise phenomenon years ago when living
In a shack near Bridgetown. Threat Level Orange,
Red just around the corner. I found one roo
Remaining in the reserve. A mob of up to eight
Have been reduced to this. Shot out or poisoned.
Bloodlust in full flow. Tyre marks on the track —
Steep, tough to negotiate — suggest enthusiasm.
The burnt-out valley is a horror to behold:
Charred chimneys of great flooded gums,
Cinders of a wedge-tailed' eyrie. Erosion
Is manifest. Here, all unravels. We must stop
It here. But 'we shall fight them on the beaches'
Is only an invitation to further damage. Instead,
Meticulously record each loss: fire, bullets, poison.
Everything outside the world they are making
For themselves on the bones of their enemies
Is watched and marked-off for erasure.
The new colonialism. They kill efficiently.
Capitalism relies on them, tooth and nail.
They can adapt to fascism or communism,
If need be. This is notification of evidence
To come, evidence gathered in the field.

Note the hard facts, note how much will stand
Up under cross-examination, how much will
Be residual, forensic and silent. As it is,
As it was, as it will be. A survey of the dead.
Young guy in white four-by-four with dual spotties
On the roof crossbar was cruising past above our block
Again: watching, studying. On Saturday I saw him
Emerge from the reserve over our crossover
Onto the Loop. He went past twice earlier today.

BOBTAIL SKELETON AT GATHERCOLE NATURE RESERVE

The form of a bobtail lizard
Tells us this puzzle of bone
And fragment of jaw with petrified
Skin and flesh, is nameable
And eternally intact. Strewn,
Though every necessary article
To rebuild the skeleton,
To conjecture the fleshiness
Of the living creature, is present.
Punch out plastic anatomical moulds
Or scored balsawood vertebrae
(Living or extinct species —
Dinosaur or Komodo dragon):
Components of tactility and magnetism;
Desire to handle, to understand
That no eyesight can ever do
As thorough a job as touch.
In the granite crevice,
Strung-out bleached white
Barren as compactness,
Exorbitant reflective heat
Sterilising and suppressing
Rot or infestation, though accelerating
The desiccation that will witness
All crumbling to dust while form
Is wilful and dogmatic.
Though still always present:
Invisible bobtail imprint,
Short stocky beast, that might

Seem three times its living length
Until a piecing-together brings it closer,
And those small leg bones
That might trick us: homunculus,
Or miniature human form
Within the form of other
Living things, eternal temptation
To be everywhere at once,
Pathetic need to keep
Assembling death's jigsaw.

ENVOY

(out of *Ex Ponto* IV, XVI lines 47-52)

Unbearable blue
crouching over
incendiary breeze
to inflict wounds
where there's no room
for further wounds;
but none compares
to loss of land
or land degraded
so even the dead
are troubled;
the malice
of profiteers
loving conversion
of land into commodities
in this golden age
of the consumer.
Iron rods in puppets.
My alienated 'belonging'.
The small choices I have.
The gall. The pall
of this western subject.
Forgive me, you
who have lost
so much more.
I sign over these words.
Ash on the page.

INSIDE

OUT

from

JAM TREE GULLY/COONDLE

IN THE TIME OF

'MOUSE PLAGUE'

AND FIRE

COMMENCEMENT: GREEN ON THE
FIREBREAKS IS TORN ASUNDER

*'To say that the poetic image is independent
of causality is to make rather a serious statement.'*
BACHELARD (*Poetics of Space, xvii*)

Shut down by a virus
My muscles have weakened.
I am slowly toning them
Into efficiency and action.
Yes, I have noticed the invasive
Green of harsh summer weeds:
Strings of 40 centigrade-plus days
Reaching into the new purple
Of 45-plus have encouraged
Burr-weeds to draw storm water
From below roads and rock ledges,
To showpony over nervous
Firebreaks. It's for all sensibilities
I am forced to find dynamic
Equivalence: people bereft
Of emotion and feeling,
Sucking it out of weeds
They hate. Recalcitrant
Hardiness evokes abhorrence
Of caltrop — it told me so.
The interference of passing
Thoughts, sibilant with soil,
Boulders, animals, the sky.
And so with a shovel
Under the damaging sun,

I make an effort to clear
Anxiety: reconnect
With the wants and snubs
Of the block, to slice
Taproots away and take
The flat green of enunciation
Out of the brutal equation.

I LOSE CONNECTION WITH WHAT I AM MOST INTIMATE WITH IF I AM NOT WRITING IT (EMERGING FROM INSIDE THE HOUSE AFTER ILLNESS)

I *understand* now, Julie! If this space
    were entirely cleared/ravaged/poisoned
(no doubt it has been in its pastoral life — we live
    in regrowth), I'd still feel connected
to its co-ordinates, its 31.5 degrees south
    and 116.4 east — and this off
a paper survey map, not a Googled act
    of *place*, a verisimilitude of decline.
It's as real and vulnerable as location, changing
    with tilt, wobbling with the strike
of an asteroid, the human heavy-hand.
    Focal point of my instinct, my genetic coding:
default setting. So emerging from house into sun,
    extending my range, intimacy is spread
back over the familiar: I *am* of, Julie, I am *of.*

NEST

'Already, in the world of intimate objects, extraordinary
significance is attached to nests. We want them to be perfect,
to bear the mark of a very sure instinct.'
BACHELARD *(The Poetics of Space)*

'There are many scales working at once . . .'
TRACY RYAN

I don't feel mocked finding an empty nest.

Found empty, after its time is done, is found at the right time.

Yes, 'delicately spun', suspended in the fork of a geranium, it defies
gravity.

The lining of down says eggs were laid, hatched, and shells kicked aside.

That though once inhabited it's too fine to be inhabited by its makers
again.

Not an annual habitat, not habitual like an eyrie.

But intense if temporary, the weaving of a small songbird.

Place of hatching and significance for parents and offspring.

Platform, repository of memory.

But no complacency where cats prowl and raptors swoop.

Close to the big house, 'our' house, a vicarious protection.

The inanimate-animate scarecrow house.

But this nest appeared in our absence.

A year overseas, as far away as one can get.

Then, *nest* was the big house, slightly under the eaves.

And now, after storms, it hangs by a thread like a milktooth.

There are no daydreams attached to this. Nothing is secured.

It hinges and flaps, and I fear for my eyesight and dreams.

An eye socket. It might look like that.

When the family flew the coop I can't say with confidence.

And I won't speak for what I didn't glimpse. No *nest* is a coop?
But experience tells me. I am keeping what I do know to myself.
Too much broadcasting can be damaging to flight.
No nest-collecting as curio, lasting only to fall from its perch, to be lost.

ROUNDING OUT THE CORNERS

Walking the block in its circular form, binding curves,
rounding out corners: a faulty deposition of belonging.

Seen through wire insecure, clearing wider firebreak fear,
policy of infliction, a self-condemnation. It's getting hotter.

This internal cornering of Royd Nook, 'great farm' chopped out,
chopped up, named after a Yorkshire nook. The small empires

of each settlement compounded. At schools here they joke
about 'nookies' behind the sports sheds, the joke carries

through to drinking age and nookies in shoddy rooms
over the bar. Laughing off those transgressions. Senses

of humour. Petty indulgences, but not 'weird' art. Only
crafts: cottage industries they hope to live off: hobbies

to income, as wet to dry. This bevelled life. Sharp corners
cushioned against impact. Pummelling the rubber buffers.

As our child grows we need fewer smooth edges, though snakes
and other wild entities (viral, animal), mean a life of rough

edges; sheltering close avenues of escape. Strainer-posts
make claim and possession; the Real Estating. Area squared

in the rounded realm; in a top corner I wrestle with the vertex
piercing my certainties and wonder if this is a measure

of a soul in modernity? How much I detect of the fast bird (a falcon?)
at forty-five degrees. Fast and slow corners. All hubris; loss.

BLACK-HEADED MONITOR LEAVES
THE ROOF SPACE AND BASKS

It's on the outside of the flyscreen door
Catching sun through beige shadecloth,
Rubbing skin on the gridwork of wire,
Its prehensile claws spread and latched:
Their own gravity. Photograph: inside out.

Outside. It has curled into a broken
Light-fitting, snug around a dead globe:
Its neck arched, it pulls in the sun.
Eye on the small entries under
Corrugated iron roofing — snugger
Than body, ribbed profile to be
Squeezed through. Photograph: threshold.

In the photo you hope to find
A hidden truth, something beyond
The naked eye. Honed. Zoomed.
Highlighted. Time to consider.
Though it's altered in the 'capture'.
The emphatic pulse in its long neck —
The distant beat of its heart.

But I was there, and memory grips.
Black-headed monitor down from
The roofspace. Rock-climber, arboreal,
Dweller of dark recesses, sun-drinker.

POUCH

When Bachelard quotes Blanchard saying,
'Fermez l'espace! Fermez la poche du Kangourou! Il y fait chaud'
We just know his experience is through news reports,
Television, literature, hearsay, zoos and/or tourism.
The same for most, unless they've ripped a joey
From the pouch after assassinating its mother.
Or pets on a farm — residue of the hunt — and children
Warming their fingers in the womb-like fold of fur and flesh.
Rediscovering origins in simulacrum. A rough guide. Gestational
    sensorium.

Or the joey: leaping headfirst into the pouch's security,
At that age transitional as the sky
With a heat-trough making sudden dark clouds,
Sudden shift in states. The boomer watching over the does
With their spare embryos, milk in their glands.
And the just-left-the-pouch — refused entry now — clinging
To the mob. The future. The boomer obsessed
With the sheath, the close feeling of skin
And moisture, of his flesh within her flesh.

That few minutes of journeying from abdomen to pouch
Is the gradation of warmth. To depart and re-enter,
To shift the threshold and to put thresholds to work.

As a child, I hand-reared a joey — bottle-feeding.
It cherished a sling of blue baby-blanket close to my chest.

The does sheltering beneath the wattles are pregnant.
Always pregnant. Their pouches are universes contracting
And expanding, testing cosmologies we struggle towards.
In this heat the idea of warmth calls for new words.

MEASURING SPACE BY CAR
(OUT OF ILLICH)

Winter dispersal of acacia blossom.
Summer dispersal of jarrah blossom.
Here, the range of wasps hunting spiders
To paralyse and lay eggs inside,
To have their larvae eat from the inside out,
Finish the job. The range of a stray bullet:
All of us at the mercy of the shooter's 'liberty'.

It's the car, here. Foot, then hoof, then wheel.
The truckie, done for driving under the influence
Walking from the pub fifteen ks up and down hills.
Sometimes he gets a lift. Without a livelihood,
He drinks his sorrows. In spite of himself,
He now knows more about where he has lived
All these years. The insects, the birds, the trees.

That's what space is: a chart of constraints.
Losing velocity and dropping quickly, metal chilling.
Space is denial or incursion, more or less.
Thornbills, weebills, red-capped robins.
Sweeps of eagles, migratory birds over-flying
To watery breeding grounds south of here.
These immense spatial configurings.

Or termites following moisture, slow spacings.
Again relative, but the marker is the damage,
As always (not glibly, not a refrain and never

A call to arms), but also a detonation. Impact.
Across the valley, piled car-wrecks.
Those cumulative years of disaster.
Pillaged for spare parts, to free up space.

PHENOMENOLOGICAL SPHERES AT JAM TREE GULLY?

You'll think how few there must be.

Ball-bearings encased in the abandoned red car —
Farm vehicle — keep spherical secrets; marooned.
The perfection of eggs of so many insect species.
Even amphibians after winter sun rises low
In the gully, though water passes rapidly over
When it comes. Water here is mainly held in tanks
Or deep underground in egg-shaped cavities;
And though at the ground's say-so, it's a crisis
Of orthography: it might prefer to be held spherically.
Is the silk sack of redback spiderlings a perfect
Sphere? Does the redback's enemy, the daddy
Long-legs, heist that sphere and drain its contents?
Round and irregular as planets if we look closely.
Is spherical intactness mere pie in the sky?
A bouncing off, a shining surface of non-interference?
For all the great stones here — ancient geology,
Acts of plutonic patience — the revelations
Of whittling down through exposure, or sedimentary-
Loss or metamorphic over-confidence, are little
Comfort. Once spheres or almost spheres but now
Egg-shaped and less. *None* I have found here
Is truly spherical. But the profusion of berries
Is a warning of nightshade: watch as fruits
Darkly elongate. No sandalwoods are left to fruit
Their tormented spheres. But I imagine spheres

Without belief or desire in perfection: the perfect
Being a tyranny and just a flaw waiting to happen.
Ball-bearings encased in the abandoned red car —
Farm vehicle — keep spherical secrets; marooned.

OUT OF THE BOTTOM DRAWER
COMES THE NEW SEED

Out of the bottom drawer comes the new seed,
a feature of *biosecurity*, a lauded breakthrough
not to be consumed by animal or plant.
Herbicide resistance in canola, as the winds
of change blow all the way from Des Moines, 1926.
I once slept next to a DuPont chemical plant
cut into a fens farm up by The Wash, and heard
its disturbed birds in my restless sleep.
Now they're seeding plants here, crazy
as overly bright canola flowers, imagined birds
who will feed on their patented genes.

Out of the bottom drawer comes the new seed,
furtive and anonymous — we locals know the signs:
biosecurity warning on a much-plied road,
heads down as visitors vanish over the hill.
It times with the bull in the uranium fields.
A canola glow is the glow of the exploited heart,
little pump driving the slightly off-key song.
Once in your head, there's no getting it out.
You'll never sing in tune again though you'll
believe you're pitch perfect. Once out, there's
no falling back into sleeps of sunshine.

Photosynthesis is a brand of sunbed.
It's an advertisement, a 'fait accompli'.
As the drying-breeze rustles through stalks

and seedpods, it is pleasantly singsong.
Who could tell the difference now the change
has come? What can be done? Enjoy the new pastoral
as locals trial their hopes, fatten to top-drawer people.
Out of the bottom drawer comes the new seed.

SPOOKED

Has something spooked the birds
Or is it just the extreme heat?
They are aghast, perched on twig and wire,
Their wings stretched and beaks open;
But nothing, only silence or the hot breeze
Fluting the cartilage of their beaks.
Yes, you can hear it if you listen,
Pick it out from the sharp silver leaves
Rustling, the ping of fencepost and wire.

Has something spooked the birds
Or is it just the extreme heat?
Searing after-effect of too many
Or too few prayers; a thirst for God
But not Godliness? What birds trans-
Mogrify out of *our* deep desire for cool,
Or to warm when cold returns? Is the sun
Distorting our vision? Are the birds similes
We latch onto within the mirage?

A pulse in Toodyay Brook:
localised swelling of the vein.
Who used to swim there,
in the blood of the great
dry heart, the vascular
watershed of dry inland?
A maintenance crew
are eating take-away
(from *where*?), perched
on the water-truck
(in case of a spark),
but a green film over
the stagnant summer
is plasma from the stoniest
of hills. Heavily shaded
by flooded-gums, it *is* a refuge.
Crustaceans, tiny fish,
beetles, all gasping for oxygen
in the thick, still blood.
Marsupials and rodents,
snakes and birds gather
to drink sunup and sundown.
It's where roads meet
and the bridge sags
under the weight
of local traffic,
and under again,
the shadows make
different life. Less confident,
less reliable life. Jets on training

flights sight off its topographical
peculiarities, a mirror
for smothered hills.
Navigating longitude
and latitude, playing off
true north and magnetic north.
So small in the larger picture;
so interconnected: as if
the rafting water-beetle
through the stygian marsh
will be swept up by a flash-flood,
the blood-thinner Warfarin,
and washed down to the river,
the sea.

BROWN FALCON: INSIDE AND
OUTSIDE THE CIRCLE

The small nest has fallen and the brown falcon
Flying from York gum to verandah rail of painted
Softwood harvested from a plantation, plantation
Where jarrah was felled to make way — jarrah
Hardwood with rings of charcoal — for pine
Trimmed to grow bolt upright, scent of resin familiar
From edges of school ovals and shaded beds of needles.

The brown falcon reconfigures according to
An empty nest: no nest-robbing, no home-breaking,
As we watch from inside our dwelling (shared
With monitors and mice in the roof, insects
And spiders), en-nested, enraptured by the head
Tilting brown falcon, as 'uncommon' *en masse*
As when I last wrote of it, though this bird
Is as familiar as its partner, our Euler diagram
Territories. We don't hunt. It peers in at us
Peering out at it, of what possession, what ownership?
Free as . . . free as changes in patterns, in displacement.

The brown falcon is one of two brown falcons
We label as one, in the circle of each other, but not
Seeing them together, at once, though infinitesimal
Specks overheard *might* be them, circling each other,
The earth. And the nest down in Bird Gully, up high,
Watching over the progress of life in all other nests,
À la carte. An imposition. But, in some ways, I am
A small bird and declare my interests. But words
Such as 'exquisite', 'remarkable' and 'magnificent'

Seed my correspondence, how I convey the sense
Of watching and being watched: through window,
Flywire door, with vocabulary stretched in the rail,
On display, vulnerable inside and out.

THINGS THAT GO BUMP IN THE NIGHT

'From goulies and ghosties and long-leggedy beasties
And things that go bump in the night
Good Lord, deliver us!'

The Cornish and West Country Litany, 1926

It's what we don't hear that disturbs most:
The tree down, wisps of smoke in a fire-ban valley,
Waking to the stench of death riding an easterly.

What are we to make of a tree down, smoke in the valley,
When neither of us has stirred, noticed inclemency?
The night tottering on as we struggle against dreams

Of waking; all those tactics of submergence
At work. Swimming and running and flying.
The sound of water gnawing: 'relieve yourself!'

Or waking after a long sleep and still feeling unwell.
Or an 'unsettled night' with no particular disruptions
To recall, dredge up, no ill winds, no creaks of a rapidly

Contracting house. But the morning is evidence.
The morning is litany and revelation, summation
And conclusion. Morning's catalogue of ships

Marooned on tinder-dry hills, the wind through the valley
A parody of their ocean. Dream readings. Deduction. Cold case.
All dogma barking at a rosy-fingered dawn. Settling

to routine, filling nocturnal folios with facts
of diurnal activity. After a while, the noise-cancelling
headphones of familiarity latch onto the ears,

Counterpoint the triumphs and failures of day,
Even where there's no energy or enthusiasm to feed them,
dragging us back to the silence, things that go bump in the night.

FROM A SMALL ROOM LOOKING OUT

for Tony in Charles Gairdner Hospital, Perth

We're back home on time to collect
Young Tim from the school bus,
Which will come winding through hills
On the crumbling road you might recollect.

He'll no doubt tell us how much he enjoys
Seeing the granites and York gums from the bus,
The house roof glinting across 'The Loop',
A mob of roos shading under jam trees.

When you visited here, we trekked
Up to the boulders, the weathered range
Opening out in its blues and purples,
Reaching north where wheat plains intersect

With slabs of burnished sky
At horizon after horizon. In
This wide place looking out,
A place of a complex and risky

Beauty, I think of you piecing
It all back together with your scientist's
Dedication to detail: each word,
Each particle of the big picture increasing

The world outside with what's in you.
From a small room looking out
We separate the wheat from the chaff,
And distance dissolves through a window.

The house huddles further into the hillside
To escape the heat, heat-stressed trees
Giving up the ghost: flyblown summer's
Growing body-count. We are still as can be
Inside the ticking house. Sudden and brutal
Expansions, metal fatigue as rooms depressurise.
In this is the mystery of stellar bodies
And the actions of gravity and dark matter.
Mystery is pure science. Waiting for night
When contractions will force us outdoors,
The house crumpling, not huddling: still hot as hell:
To be hurled out over the hills and plains,
Marking new points on the compass:
Trees struggling on, suckers reaching up
Out of burnt stumps and rootstock.
So dry we fear only the effect of rain:
The dread of surprise, the violent results.

CENTRED

(i)

While
you're at home
being independent
the gaggle at shire chambers
meet and make
local decisions and you fall
into their locality;
so when machinery rolls by
on the top road and the bulldozer
topples the last great tree
you'll rebuke yourself:
if you'd been there, they wouldn't
have listened
and would have cast their vote
just to hurt,
to topple even more
if at all possible.

(ii)

Watching
the beginning and end
of the *Wizard of Oz*
I stayed in Kansas: earthbound
and stormwracked among people
I know: I remember
the curious wet nose of a terrier:
my childhood, another world,
where inland met the sea.

(iii)

The hot sun
so close and at full pitch;
basking in the afterglow of meteorite-burst
and the close passing of a lumpen asteroid,
the hills lined with early
morning viewers, I toss and turn
and stay indoors, muggy,
fitful,
but though the glare hurts
I stare out into the blue
and see stars stretching daylight
far back far away
and the trajectory
of all asteroids —
what's every forty or twelve-hundred years?
what's every Sodom or Gomorrah?
what's every Tunguska,
every catastrophe fetish
to one who denies
the passage of time,
the stretch, the distancing,
breaking point and collapse,
who increasingly forgets
what was said
just a moment
ago?

(iv)

'this false genre'
BACHELARD

Daydreaming
this false genre — the hill so steep
when a virus pulls your strings,
splays you over gravel's slippery slide:
no staircase will last if cut
from the mixed media
hillside,
the wash eating soil footings away,
rocks free-floating,
steps tumbling down onto steps.
Keep your horns in,
waving them about
won't get you anywhere,
and when the mob come over the crest,
breach the granites and hack up the soil,
it'll be too late —
on top of you before
you can *pull your head in.*
As Dad used to say?

(v)

'earth in the words'
TALKING LANGUAGE (WITH ERNIE DINGO)

The elders will talk if you approach them.
They are omnipresent. It's not retrospective.
It's now. Listen listen. Stories of place.
Them. We. You. I. All.

COMATOS AND LACON

How likely is it that the fellas who have
moved onto a place down the loop, who
are bricking their crossover, are named
Comatos and Lacon? That they have
brought a small herd of goats with them,
and play guitars outside their house-shed
as the summer sun is setting purple on the hills?
If I say, It's entirely true! will you believe
that they are more than mythology,
that the sweat they drop onto the hillside
will erupt into an army of teeth-gnashers,
that they will join ranks and roll into
the brook and down into the river
and on to the sea? That oceans will rise
because of them? And what if I add,
It's in your best interest to believe
because this is the only reality left
to us, that even up here with great
plains spreading below us, oceans
of tears will soon be lapping at our feet,
and the goats will bleat their warning.

Delayed gratification — the explorer's big pay-off.
Social adulation starbursts all that loneliness
(witness/diary/television cameras), with those
uppity assistants and fellow-travellers wanting in,
hogging a flash of limelight: no way, José!
Their bold tentative tautological oxymoronic steps
were ultimately economic which is the mainstay
of the kitbag. Even mountains pay off for a time
in the end before the end. In their Explorer Clubs
they high-five *and* look brooding. Insular,
possessed, frostbitten, parched, far-away-eyed.
Because-it's-there, horizons, last frontiers, endeavour.
It's so lexical emerging from the silence. So much
happier away, but others must follow in wakes
to confirm, to lift it from the fantastical (realms).
Homing beacon, reporting back, supreme attention
deficit in trade-route pathfinding: they passed here
in the Nook high in saddles, muskets primed.
Insecular godheads scout portents and sailors
and waves of water, sand, jungle, rock: oil
companies kissing their feet, human aspirations
and personifications lingering collective memory,
passed on by skin of mouth, even rumours
served. First to cross in white skin, first to blacken
the record highlighting complexion as goggles
reflect back the harsh elements, the relics
strategically placed to immortalise death.

ROOTS

Watering the young eucalypts will mean their roots
Reach up, grow to the light, the particles of moisture;
And when surface-water is absent, there'll be no deep-
Searching roots to nourish or water the sapling, the tree.

It's a tipping-point, the lower leaves drying and falling,
That straggling look, that vulnerability to high winds
Or storm. How long to hold out? Howling for a downpour
When a downpour might knock them out; tip into death.

Thunder woke me. Dry lightning flashed
Through the blinds. I stayed awake in vigil.
Fire comes at such times. In such *conditions*.
What do you do with a word like 'perfect'?
Shows its colours? Reveals itself for what it is?
There are occasional spots of rain. A brief shower
Almost gasoline on dry ground, bush as tinder.
Water conducts electricity. It does, *doesn't it.*
Weary, I smell the burning and see the bloody
Smoke through the verticals, the storm clouds
Not working perfectly. As sentinel I grow sleepy,
At this of all times. Watching over family,
Peering out from the dark into the ghastly
Intermittent light that serves us awake, asleep.

FEVER POEM

Last autumn's plantings are on their last legs: deep seeking roots
Need watering and the tree's system cooling. They are in their
Dry fever, and I zigzag the hillside delivering water to footholds.
A brown falcon lands on the top firebreak and stalks over to scrape
At the damp, break out the moisture. It eyes what clings to its talons.
An adolescent. Bachelard would maintain it in its anxiety, its fear.
The transmutational qualities of the moment. Mirages clinging
To ground so much hotter for water: the brief, intense steaming.

Indoors, young Tim has scarlet fever — unusual at ten and in this era.
That scourge of life and literature before antibiotics: the stressed metaphor.
Death stalks pioneers at their lonesome outposts; their spirits fall
Onto the land like dry ice. Such creativity, this raging of the brain.
Paths taken and lost, the temporal and spatial mileposts. Within
Tim's head is the journey as we watch at his bedside, or step
Out amongst the feverish trees, their brown hawk. Now, steam
Is the scarlet sunset that will bring the black, starless night.

FREEING A MOUSE FROM
THE HUMANE TRAP AROUND MIDNIGHT

Towards midnight, I set out across the block
with a mouse in the 'humane trap': to release
into a moonless dark, up near the western fence,
among granites and fallen trees, dry and whittled-
back by the sun, wind, and entropy: refuges
for the little grey tremblers transferred from the house
in this time of 'mouse plague' — an abundance
of mice in roof and walls, running the frame,
reminding me of childhood and the farm
when panels in outbuildings collapsed
under the weight of field-mice boiling over,
or when lifting a sheet of corrugated iron
from the ground sent grey sparks flying
in all directions after strange attractors:
not chaos, but a perfect illustration
of transitivity, rapid dispersal with micro-
decisions made according to threat
and geography, what was known and what
was aberrant. So, walking the stony hillside,
torchlight wavering in one hand, trap in the other,
a strong wind dulling the senses, threatening
to bring down overhanging branches,
a vertigo of expectation: the predictable
(a route in daylight I have walked so often)
with the unknown, what darkness throws
to change the course of a life, my life, the mouse's.
So, walking the stony hillside, I operate within
safety limits, can tread with reasonable doubt
while being cautious, but approaching

the wire fence into the reserve, anxiety
and vertigo increase and a strange test-
case is pushed to the extreme. I tell myself
that this has nothing to do with 'property',
but everything to do with boundaries.
That's what's familiar and why it's familiar.
So, walking the stony hillside, I grow more
disorientated. Sensing the boundary,
I free the mouse. I understand its attempts
to hop back into the trap before embracing
torchlight and staring me down, turning tail
and racing towards the wire, the pitch-black.

RELEASING THE MICE:
ZONES OF HELL

In my morning traipse across the block
west sou' west, through granite gnarls
and fallen logs, clutching the humane
trap with its kick inside, to scissor
over wire fence into the reserve, trace
the roo trail and breach the rise
to the outcrop of split rock thick
with lichen, where I release mice
to give them the best chance
against the shire's pathological
autumn burn after the fire season
trails off: the jack-in-the-box spring
of a field mouse as it plays space
to diminish openness, to zero a crack,
then finding a dead end, dart out
to attempt another, then disappear.
But the mouse's liberty is parodied
by rifle shots fracturing the air. Rapid-fire,
high-calibre, something almost military.
I'll catch a stray slug while *liberating*
this mouse, caught in the deathwish.
On buying 'humane traps', Tracy was told:
'leave them all in there to eat each other,'
and John, in another wheatbelt town,
was instructed: 'just drop it in a bucket
when you've caught a few, and let
them drown.' I walk steadily, predictably,

back to 'our' fenceline, but my heartbeat
hastens until I scissor back over; my pulse
starts to slow: a loss of pressure, as though
I have been hit, life ebbing away.

U-TURNS

I remove two more mice and take them up to the fence
by the arena. Gladiatorial, but not like Australian troops
in Afghanistan as described by their own senior officer
(I know them, they dwell out here before and after enlisting).
I learn that mice will always go with the wind: if I let them
out facing into it they'll U-turn over my boots and rush
further than the wind will carry them, as far as shelter.

TEST CASE

Their shit is — sorry, their 'droppings' — are everywhere:
in the books, the cupboards, the bedrooms; they pull
at fabric and chew grouting between the tiles
when food sources are cut off; I release dozens
from tubes. Like humans, they are powerful vectors
for nematodes, ringworms, viruses, bacteria;
such short intestinal tracks can even brew tapeworms;
and when 'plague conditions' are ripe, they fall victim
to politics. Are these mixed messages? As Berkman says
in his *Prison Memoirs of an Anarchist*: 'My space is all.'
So is theirs. Government websites warn of mental
erosion in the *grand mal* compassion: exterminators
suggest making them bleed slowly inside. We persist
with our 'humane' methods, sleepless and driven crazy
by all other stresses, the shit — the droppings — of life,
of collective conviction, determination to do things right.
What heroes: to none, *not even* to the mice.

WADDLE

Early morning mouse release (you walk away from the song
of the insomniac owl, his blinkered challenge to sunrise)
and an echidna sudden in an open space between jam trees,
flat to the slope, beak sticking out sense-laden but rigid as long-
cooled volcanic rock. It is a large, mature creature and its bristles
are forests of incinerated trees, catching slivers of fresh sunlight
through thin leaves, this owl's slow progress to sleep, demi-hunt
of half-wakefulness. Echidna seems sick or sluggish, if not deceased,
but you know that's what you're supposed to think. You move past
without much obvious interest, freeing the mouse
up near the arena where it springs into the hellfire of daylight,
summer ground already burning; it darts into a dark split
in granite. You don't have to turn back to know the echidna
will have made rapid progress, 'waddling' downhill, resisting
termite-rich fallen branches, though scratching to mark
them for an evening return. Its beak held high, sniffing air,
ground, essence of morning. Quills much more than armour,
shimmering. You can't help but watch its tactical retreat, and brace
in expectation of the hill thundering, shaking beneath your boots.
So liquid and yet conclusive. The owl shuts down completely
as the sun takes over and echidna quills shoot their last dark rays
before going to earth. Starkly awake, you retreat indoors.

MICE NESTING IN THE HOUSE:
STOVE, WALLS, ROOF, ROOMS

The fall-thru from ceiling vent
to tiled floor is an act of irresponsible
courage and pragmatism: what else can we say?
The nightly drop produced a wanderer,
a scrabbler for outdoors or, better still, roof
and wall cavities where well-trodden paths
nourish the needs and desires of life.

Building a new nest in a toy's cavity
or a drawer or a box of papers pulped
to service the nest: these litters of babies
pink and vulnerable as childhood struggles
to be child *and* parent, build the present
and future into an act of warmth, nurturing.
Explaining the politics of caring is hard.

Maintain equilibrium and determination.
Pattering over the ceiling to play up
your heavens, the roof over your head,
knitting your lousy dreams together
or the nightmare of the mouse bursting
alien-like out of your chest, then
picking you down to the bone.

Architecture is part of the psychology:
shelter a lapse into *primitive* urge:
the more intricate the plans, the more
desperate the builders to succeed:

basic principles, mythologies, concrete
house-pad, sand underbelly: cake
and eating it. Crumbs drawing them in.

The abject scuttle: drawn as veins
through our bodyhouse: shucked skin
we sweep out, exfoliating. Scrabbling away.

THREATENED

This is how small it can get: inside, protecting
ourselves against mice and bathos. Minuscule
but overwhelming. And outside — exterior —
with its massive threats and sharp angles,
its great weights, able to reach in as efficiently
as mice, though without the politeness
of small openings, vestigial entries: in fact,
one can go out on a limb, hang on a thread,
find one's way back on the breadcrumb trail
and bring the terror of what's out there back in.
In essence, I am already 'dead & buried'
in a neighbour's eroded firebreak, sliding
through every crack in my new, ghost-self,
yelling warnings though no one knows how
to listen, to hear me. Today, I *was* threatened.
I brought it back in with me. I can't see the text
I am typing. At sundown, mice will still scurry
through the roof, *searching searching*. We let
them live: they are my best side. No harm done?

SEALED IN / BLOCKED OUT

The last drop zone, last hole lost to the corner
of an old built-in wardrobe: free-falling mice
with no way back. No death-defying. No complete
annihilation of gravity. A fright night for young Tim
as they forced their way in, all other entries
finally tracked and sealed. And now this portal
blocked with steel wool and plaster. Each night
we sit and listen to the scurrying and fretting
at old entries: behind the stove, around laundry
pipes, behind cupboards. They work in teams,
in shifts, but don't break through. But there
are vague, diminished spaces where thought
is lost to anxiety: around window frames, points
where glass doors slide over glass walls, soft-
points where gyprock might be gnawed open.
But for five mornings now, the humane traps
have remained empty. The neurotoxic waft
of peppermint oil is fading with a hot breeze
that still finds entry points too thin, too small
even for mice. Sealed in, we've almost blocked
the world out — world that would come rushing,
forcing a way through dreams and brief silences.
How far into our heads have the mice burrowed?
Do we carry them inside out with us, everywhere?
Black-shouldered kites are in the ascendant
and watch us closely: hovering over paddocks,
any place mice would merge into the open.
We know that prey and pray are not homophones,
but precisely the same word. Things that sound
alike are one and the same: the silence of a diving

and a falling kite, the heart excited and terrified:
awaiting the small feet running over the ceiling,
expectation of an entry missed, a new incursion.
Or a weakness imagined, detected and made good.

Mice do not go lightly, they have the heaviest step.
Back in the house, we hear them at all hours: wearing
grooves into plaster ceilings, running the steelwork of walls.
But they can't get in. From their inside to our inside.
It's become a world of separation, of distinct belongings.
It's our wish, not theirs. They have proved their willingness to mingle.
A month in the tropics, on an island so high it might topple,
and the mice here settled into their exclusion, their new routines.
Outdoors, evidence is everywhere. In the red shed. In the silver shed.
Removing the covers of exhaust fans in the house, to cover with flywire
to prevent mouse shit raining down on our heads as reminder,
as punishment? A mouse pokes its head through the open porthole
and looks to drop in on our otherworld confidence. For the life
of it, it can see no reason for the divorce, no reason for our uppitiness.

The wheatbelt is acquiring its green tinge — each year we fear
it will never come again. And the cruel are out there killing roos
with arrows snapped off near hearts. Violent weekend parties
calling time on nature in the valley. On the other side of the country,
Queensland farmers are chomping at remnant bushland. That's regional
and that's national: accumulation of like-mindedness. Like mining:
it leaves nothing for anyone. Not even the sighting of a night parrot
will stop a mine. And certainly not people's rights. And mice
are part of the equation. Unwanted. Turned back. Up to their 'antics'.
Mice do not go lightly, they have the heaviest step.

INSURANCE POLICY

A last humane trap set as insurance policy.
Fresh peanut-paste at the back of the flattened
circumflex that will tip and shut its mouth if a mouse
goes for the bait. But for nights it has remained
untouched, untipped. No mouse is likely
to resist that long. Is it hubris to suggest
that I have learnt the psychology of mice?
Or at least their tendencies and weaknesses?
To say that fresh peanut-paste is temptation:
that it is a 'wicked delight', or a 'devastating
dessert', or a 'divine act', lifted to a finer plane?
In times of 'plague' we develop our humour?
But we've won out: the fruit can breathe easier
in the fruit bowl, the crumbs not gathered
from beneath the table. Incredible forces
keep the trap upright and open, deep in
where the bait smoulders untouched.
Insurance policies rely on odds falling
in their favour. In their dead hearts
nothing gnaws at the core of wealth.
Our barely mutual living space.

READING THE FADING TEMPLATES

I saw the strips of bark on the paving slabs
before they were swept away: the swirling tannin-like stains
are markers that in fading make a wide range of templates:
plough marks fading in unploughed paddocks do the same.

Depending on the accuracy of seeing, finesse of sight,
you can see a long way back. You find template on template.
Such anxiety, such influence. It can be put to work in all sorts
of ways, with all sorts of intentions. And what is brought here

via the brain is the same: stain of tropical vegetation:
palm fronds from Cocos Islands, tamarinds from La Réunion:
a composite across time. The tropical stain and wash-away.
The deluge at Jam Tree Gully while we were absent

set everyone hoping the season had set in with a vengeance:
its assault on shifting climate, on responsibility (to do more / to do the same),
to embrace the refrain, to lust after the cyclical again, again. Strips
of bark were drenched and ran their contents, staining pavers,

then the roof leaked and we returned to repairs. On
La Réunion, the highest daily rainfall ever recorded wasn't
long ago. Though the west coast of the island around St Gilles
is comparatively dry — some say only fourteen days of rain a year.

Water is pumped from the luxuriant east to grow sugar cane
on the west. All of that comes to mind. Quarantine is memory-loss.
The customs of one place and their templates. What's allowed through.
Stains we erase and lose, stuff not even hinted at here.

THE LOCAL STRUGGLES TOWARDS
A MULTICULTURAL NOTION OF PLACE

If a lot has been written about this, it's not much evident out here.
Out here — go and unpack that! The praying mantis on the wall
is respected by few — the sprayers are out to kill off the slightest
evidence of unsolicited green poking through desiccated earth.
Rain excites then angers them. Origins are ironed out and the local
works its codes through the national mythology. Whiteness
is an absence they want to fill with more whiteness. All else
is infiltration. A fringe is referenced when there's no stopping it.
Difference is minority and can be tolerated with sharp jokes,
like plough tines or spray nozzles. Plough tines or spray nozzles?
'Get back home' or 'Fuck off, we're full' (speaking for the ALL,
the THEM, the US), bothers a slight increase in reference
to earlier occupants in town museums and on shire websites —
how magnanimous, how sensitive. Opening the door they
slammed shut. Who are we talking about in the salient blue?
Metempsychotic spray making rainbows over Poison Hill,
just down from Mount Toxicity, to the unravelling of credentials
in the swirl, the valley mixing-bowl where ingredients refuse
to gel, though some do, wanting their own cake and their own
way of eating it too, which will be your way if you want to SURVIVE
in most localities, in the eyes of most collectors of killed insects,
temporary in glassine envelopes. Speech of indignant exclusion
is in short, sharp spurts, almost anecdotal, or in furious diatribes
that frighten quieter people. Values adding brand-named citizens.

Fire costs. Flame has rights.
Stacked vegetation set alight
without nurture or warmth
as a raison d'être.

The charring grey in green nimbus,
the burning of sap running faster,
the acrid measurement of indulgence:
nothing grows well in choked air.

Regeneration reaches for its catheter,
it springs an enthusiasm for burning:
every little fire that might be lit,
smoke signals from afternoon television.

Taking what they want
from the 'authentic':
which way the smoke blows
and brings fallout to clothes

hung out to dry,
working clothes, leisurewear,
pragmatic and barely sustainable
beyond the erotic and even then, temporary.

Fire in their gussets.
Fire burning prolifically
as the fire-risk season passes
and the bans are lifted.

A shorter burning-off season than ever
but nothing will stop them cramming it in.
Fresh air is smoke. The new purity.
Annealed to lungs, aspirations.

Fire costs. Flame has rights.
Stacked vegetation set alight
without nurture or warmth
as a raison d'être,

inside burning out.

TRAP

Diverter. First-flush device. Trap for the slurry of dust and debris,
bird shit and the casings of hatched insect pupae, washed from roof.
If you miss the first rains and your trap hasn't been cleared,
all of these become one with your water, one with you.
But good housekeeping has you letting the flush cascade
out of the diverter, straight from its mouth — no 'shut your trap!'
but 'speak freely', a gush of water and matter down over the hillside.

So far, so good. But then you're away, and there's a long gap
between showers, and the crap builds again but the trap is full
and next to no flush for what's washed down from the roof
into gutters into pipes into the great ninety-thousand litre tank.
You've been caught out by dirt and boot-prints from roof repairs
(that rough weather just before leaving), and the filth makes its way
down into that large percentage of what will be you one way or another.

Towards midnight last night, the rain came again, and though you'd
been caught out why compound the problem? You went out and opened
the trap by torchlight and watched your anxiety gush downhill, cutting
its way between rocks and trees, and vanish into the hazy rain-filled
    darkness.
Your feet unsteady on soft ground, perched up there trying to screw
the cap onto the pipe, telling yourself that there was so much to play for
in this game of living — though never a gambler, never a profiteer.

But it's not necessary to lose, is it? And humility is the mopoke singing
dirges to wet leaves in its adagio as you tread down along the alien fenceline,
torchlight splintering off rain and making false light part of you
as much as water in the tank, altering who you are and who you will be.

Truth is, you don't want to be out in the wet and the cold, struggling half-blind and off your chosen course, head filled with impurities. But you weren't going to be diverted from your task with so much to play for.

VATIC

Flashbacks bring no visions.
Colourful parrots elicit
no bloody reckonings,
the past dragged across oceans
and transplanted: others
have snapshots that flourish,
but we can no longer
reach them.

Flashbacks bring no visions.
Christ ended up a figurehead
of a blood sacrifice religion.
Today, they drive distances
to worship him. Would they listen
beyond pennies to heaven,
if prayers for lush crops
were forbidden?

Flashbacks bring no visions.
Senses open to opportunities:
ear out, eye out, nose
to the ground. Is that a new
air-seeder Jack's got? Are
yellow capeweed flowers
spinning about dead
centres?

Flashbacks bring no visions.
Some will kneel and some
will donate. Watch tractors

keel-haul such pleasant land.
So many white-faced herons:
more than a handful. And
farms dams suddenly,
astonishingly replenished.

Flashbacks bring no visions.
In dead spaces of cities
prism of oil to light the firmament.
Eye to eye. Down the barrel.
Passing out of the semi-rural
vision focuses through clouds
and plumes: spray-nozzle
legacy. Barrelling the roads.

Flashbacks bring no visions.
Nurtured and wrapped
in the spectrum of place,
some eye the great eagles
without resentment.
Inside out. Leaving
a feather where it falls.
Taking note.

Flashbacks bring no visions.
World intense in a handful of dirt.
Bees grid the block, working
their way up: a hum is mistaken:
the trough has passed, stormless.
Corella outside its flock
a frantic daylight angel.
Flourishing still-life.

FROG DECLARATIVE

Near the northernmost tip of their 'range',
pinpoint of habitat, yellow-flanked burrowing frogs
have burst into presence on the floor of the valley
where heavy rains have disturbed stale red earth
and brought bloody-white flow to the channel
carved through granite; the contra-indicative hoots
of owls we hear most nights — no imitation with no human
in their owl-talk — working forlorn lost-soul messages
for we know not what. Instead, full choir — *no*, that reeks
of the mating brawl of emergence, and the boosted buzz
of the humming frog carrying uplands further than it should,
and the squelch of Gunther's toadlet dragging itself over rocks.
Rather, all varieties in this vicinity cross-talking, honed
as erosion, honed as the will to spawn and call out about it.
Water doesn't hold long in channel in its tilt to brook and river,
but long enough in pools for follow-up rains to have a say.
Frogs in decline are shouting out for the slightest depth,
frogs in decline declare their willingness to co-operate.

BELOW THE GRAFT

Below the graft
suckers appear liberally
and reach up fast,
exponential growth
so impressive
with first rains
that you delight
in the citrus finally
taking hold, that fruit
might appear years
ahead of its time.
But these suckers
are from tough rootstock,
vigorous but small
fruiting, if fruiting at all:
this is the kind of lesson
morality would have us
apply to our surroundings.
Cut back enthusiasm;
control the wild base stock;
favour the slower growth
of the refined stock on top.
Whole cultures have sucked
this bitter lemon. And yet,
denying them all,
I accept the shoots
being removed,

almost rubbed off,
as if they never were,
leaving the vigour
to subterranean
movement.

GREGARIOUS NOT GREGORIAN

Despite reclusiveness
much knowledge comes
from contact: the guru's
pragmatic visits yield
many more words than words
said, and the echoes of an action
resonate long after the gate
is closed, the Gregorian
darkness sets in.

RAMS AND THE RED SHED

(i)

First, about the light. It was a couple of weeks ago
but the light was similar to this afternoon's; though now
the sun is lower and it's a few days from the equinox.
Light is never really the same. Looking outside late afternoon
and the sun is overriding the segmentation of the metal rhomboids
of the top gate: though looking into the contradictions long enough
has the wire melting into the light. It's *only* about light here,
the wash and awash of muting colours. Light is what takes
me back to the two rams 'lost' or hiding or taking cover
in the far south-western corner of the block, two weeks ago.
Lost or escaped. Driven or transplanted. 'Sam' pounded on
our door while we showered until he got activity, staring
in through curtains, taking mental notes. 'My rams are on
your block,' he says. 'I hope they don't eat my tree saplings,'
I say, after Tracy has taken in the picture. 'They're not my rams,'
he volte-faces, staring past me deep into the house. I pull
the door closed behind me, his eye beams bouncing off
and falling back into the yard. I can tell this will be the start
of a grand narrative, of time and place and psychology,
of old ways and modernity, of the many isms just beneath
the surface; a rejection of separations. 'Look, mate, I'll call
the ranger to help me round them up later — I will see they
make their way *home*.' 'They won't eat the saplings, not
with the grass up like that. They prefer grass to saplings,'
he says, moving from foot to foot. I think, 'All goes awkward
and outward, nothing collapses.' I don't offer to help him now —
half-dressed, I need time to adjust to the light. I need Sam gone.

Two young rams — one a merino, the other a poll dorset. Almost peas
in a pod; massive ball-sacks and testosterone to stare you down like the sun,
you being the open gate, the gate just waiting to melt away. All that
ethnology of sheep shadowing people and their crisis of 'variety'. The woolly
folds (survival) of the merino, the 'meat sheep' poll dorset, balls a passport
to life. But brothers in rebellion and distress: small horns on one, the other
hornless, charging when cornered, it has to be said, brothers-in-arms.
I won't impose a pacifism on them, stuck as I am in tropes of masculinity.
I herd them, I encourage them, I plead and cajole, I steer them towards
the open door of the red shed; a set-up. In there they can make hay in half-
light until the ranger arrives with the float to collect and cart them to their
'owner — the 'Not-Sam'. But corralled, with Tracy and me herding and
    herding,
Ya Yahing! and Whoo Whooing!, get along now get along, up and down the block,
in and out of the saplings, following the lines of wild oats, the grass,
    zigzagging
heading off blocking guiding encouraging, 'Sprouting alike in broad zones
and narrow zones.' I am remembering back a few months now: the visceral
actions, the poem as long as time. When this all began. The rounding,
the rounding up. But it's supra-vivid and this post-storm light is right
in some ways and wrong in others; it evokes at an angle, a tangent to event,
and the rams hurry into the shed but Merino, to name names, charges back
past us before the door slides shut. Poll Dorset can be heard butting the metal
and snorting. The ranger is coming with the float. We work to keep Merino
(we're on first name terms now!) on the block as its eyes narrow to wire and
    light;
stamping hooves and baaing loudly to its comrade it signals something
beyond our understanding, then it's off for the top of the block, to force
its way under the wire and away. Light folds in on itself. A black hole.
What *were* its parting words? 'We'll meet again by the light of the moon . . .
in the shade of a different shed in a different place . . . ?' The ranger pens

the trapped poll dorset into the float. No sign of the escapee. We guess
at its homing instinct, we determine qualities of light in which to tell the tale,
and the ranger points to her bruises made by another ram on another day.

AN ABSENCE OF GHOSTS

An absence of ghosts
is a shocking prospect:
being many colours
of transparency.
Darkness forms lines
around our warmth
attracting night creatures:
moths, owls, and mice.
Ghosts we'd prefer
not to discuss. But we're
in pain when we lack
their touch. And they
will go so easily —
all at once — at night,
or in daylight.

PORTRAIT OF THE POET AT FIFTY
(AT JAM TREE GULLY)

'le sot Matisse'

The white-haired fear of smoke
curling back into the house
through the open window
while dark cloud that will
produce no rain taunts
the green weedy sheen
of the valley walls. Such smoke
is a jolt of memory,
the burning base of an old
fencepost no doubt once treated
in creosote — carcinogen, though
depleted and failing in the striations
of age, the reaching-through
of moisture and decomposition
lessening the surface area,
the subterranean plot. Still,
you don't burn them by choice —
this got scooped up in the tailings
of the woodpile and, tossed onto
hot coals, was beyond retrieval.
Fumes rising the firebox door
sealed shut. Windows thrown
open; no, closed. Truth and anxiety
in equal measure, a tendency
to skin irritations and a lessening
obsessiveness (you'd claim
the sensible bit remains).

Wanting to paint in colours
without the burn they carry,
addicted to the light
though seeing most words
lit-up in the dark.
Birds are the soundtrack.
You live among those
who think you're the village
idiot. And you find comfort
that his homepeople said
the same of Matisse.
Clutching at straws,
the whitening stubble,
remnants of summer.

THE DECORATIVE ARTS:
GROWTH AND EXTERMINATION

Trees planted for concord
make a garden where bush
recently flourished; growth
of ornaments a sculptural
assertion; or the 'feral'
dog in among the sheep,
and the bottom-of-the-valley
hobby farmer 'having to shoot' *it*
because it's a dangerous decoration
or a dangerous redecorator,
because it is as much as he is?

CUTOUTS AND LIGHT (AFTER MATISSE)

Fill the window with cutouts.
They vary by the second. Time
is their main ingredient, their shape
is colour: of bark, of grass, of sand,
of clay, of rock, of sky, of fence,
of beetle, of fly, of bird. They
are interwoven cuttings of colour.
All colour is contact but nothing
is primary. In cutting out
and filling this window, prevent
slivers and shapes of island
blocking out what's immediately
at hand. It's a lot to do with time,
as said. It has a socio-political
dimension. Fronds of coconut palms,
waterfalls, sea meeting sky.
But predominantly violet,
from which you slice clouds,
with no rain, or so much rain.

HOLLOW(ING)

When the sun hollows shadow or hollows rain showers
themselves having hollowed the burnt sienna playing
colours; hollow is endearment, hollow is richness
and fullness; where the wind opens hollow it isn't
erosion but transference, new forms come out
of this hollowing; it is nurturing and parallel,
it co-exists as sings out when hollow logs burn
in the firebox and their cries pipe many agonies
and joys, ecstasies and pains; in the hollows
heaviness is lightness and light holding the weight
of the world up without difficulty; the hollows here
hold their makers and opportunists (not a negative,
here it's good fortune unless something is driven out
then a more complex picture arises and hollows
become James I via Marx calling beggars vagabonds/rogues
when I'd still like to think it's because they haven't
worked the ethics of hollows, of sanctuary: none
should be whipped, including the whippers themselves);
machinery shaking hollows through the valley shocks
and there are few if any Marxists about, children starting
the pumps and hiding out — when the mining boom passes
will children become enslaved to their fathers' needs to progress?
Or is hollow survival against the odds — rout of the devout?
Spiders cast hollows in broader spaces, funnels of black
house spider, a trap so necessary; or trapdoors opened
by wasps that drag spiders from hollows to their muddy
chambers; and the antlions down low with their pits,
their perfect hollows, those cones from inverted, rounded
pyramids more cosmic than alignment with stars
through leaves, though I noticed them warp

with the super moon, ital urge buckling
the whole planet, antlions' jaws buckling
as the sand falls, the hollows cave-in.

VENUS

Venus through daylight
burns stronger than the sun
which you can't focus on.
The blue of day is a screen
behind which all night
shelters. You can pattern
a life around it, fixate.
Nothing is lost. I starwatch
looking away from the sun,
but at the brightest times.
Love is just another variable,
but its bright inkwork
through branches gives
sparkle to myths.
Passionals carry sufferings,
lights in the sky you fail
to recognise or identify.

ECOLOGY AND THE WOODHEAP
AND THE 'ION' SUFFIX

There is plenty of room for misunderstanding forms.
There were the trees — attended by dirt, insects and small reptiles —
transferred from wholeness to segments, then piled in a heap.
This is no neat stack, which might come later. This is the toss-off,
the hurl, the rawshock accumulation, the home fires that will burn
without consideration of what kept the home upright.
So many contradictions and ambiguities in the spaces between —
how much more is occupied by randomisation, the higgledy-
piggledy, stressing and casualness of space. The paradox
of the woodheap and the ecology that sets in when less
is lifted off or none at all because warm days (fuelled
in part by the smoke rising from the hearth) mean it's left
as is. Winter lizards resettle and some on the aberrant sun-days
make their way across for a better place to persist with hibernation,
ants scouring for skin cells and body parts to cart away. All
incinerations are resplendent in the potential of the heap,
as if this is something to glory over, when it's not. It never is.
So many ramifications, so much history that rushes past,
gone up in flames. Our unsteady relationships with elements
we praise, the perverse comfort of a woodheap large enough
but not too large, all that fallen wood gathered together
that might have been shaped into a meeting-house
to suit us all if only it could be kept warm
without consuming itself, warm enough
on the remaining cold nights left to us.

SÉANCE MEMORY AND COLD SO BITTER THAT THE FIRE IS KEPT BURNING DESPITE CONSEQUENCES TO THE BIOSPHERE

The polypipe T-junctioning off the housepipe
from the tank via the pump has split with the cold:
the valley freezing after the searing of summer.
I think of the pipes iced in minus 20 in Mt Vernon, Ohio,
and the basement flooding with the thaw, the agony
we paid for in so many ways; freezing in the house,
blankets piled ridiculously high, trying to keep baby
warm between us — at Tracy's breast to suckle
body warmth. I have just done a patch-up job —
cutting the split pipe away, rejoining, but without
plumber's tape in this cold weather, the joint won't seal
and there's a steady dripping away of our life's blood.
Water we worship. Which takes me to the séance,
the ouija board when we were in my girl-cousin's bedroom,
and the glass spelling what needed to be spelt in that over-
darkened space (blankets on windows to prevent moonlight
on our faces, though a torch shone sickly over the spirits'
orthography), extracting spectres from everything
to hand. And then to America again, to James Merrill's
changing light. The glass skips about the letters
and spells a name: Wilderness. Then: False. And:
Celebration. Last night I stayed up late, too late,
to keep the fire burning through to the cold of first light —
Tim unwell, and minus 4 on the cards. The risk of freezing pipes.
Possibilities play themselves out in noises and light
of flame. Tim says he wants the dreams he fears so much.
And he a child who loves the dark, can't bear even
a sliver of moonlight. The extra warmth in this cold

winter house is passage to the formless world of sleep:
more active than any glass searching out
words to claim, words to speak of.

WHY I LET OTHER LIVING THINGS STAND MY GROUND AND HOW THE INORGANIC CAN BE LIVING, TOO

In my small pinched vision of the world,
one in which little activity counts for a lot
and consequences are manifest and multiply,
I let other living things stand my ground
and witness the inorganic as living, too.
My focus dwindles to the effect and affect
of a square metre, and how that metre
can never be contained: how the split rock
increases the surface for lichen, that deep below
another rock is made. I see birds diminished
in their singing tree, I hear colours drain
from consistent skies, or worse, in the little
space I stare into, flaring to announce things
will pass, all our clichés be laid to rest.

YES, I AM CALLING YOU A RACIST, WALT WHITMAN. PURE AND SIMPLE.

'Flow my tears, fall from your springs.'
JOHN DOWLAND

Nation obsessed with intactness and not the cost to others.
Each 'solution' diminishes and raises earth's temperature.
The thermometer is broken and we can only guess how close
to the line we are. The precisions of science fall with the feather.

When light fails or can't work through, trying too hard maybe,
the jiddy-jiddy in the oldest jam tree signs me in and rightly
expects to be followed — my ears are attuned to irregularities
in the ground, more than I know are there, the bumps and crevices
you'd never see no matter how strong the light, how long you stare.

I note that two properties — two neighbours of small holdings —
up the valley must have combined forces, joined hands to plough
across fencelines and survey pegs to make one crop to be shared.
Okay, but they've also annexed part of the reserve land and expanded
their Spartan kingdom. All will pay for their Thermopylae.

So watching what goes on over our fences is intrusive. Believe you me,
they do the same, damning each tree planted in the abstract (as they see it).
What I cling to isn't upturned earth but a tree, clinging as the hillside
erodes away. I hear abstract nouns though I keep them back.

Out the corner of my eye I see Van Gogh swirling olive trees
in the paddock gallery, straight from New York under auspices.
I saw real olive trees thriving on gallery walls: grown locally.
The curatorial implosion is every step I make in alien familiarity.

But despite micro-observations, only this morning I discovered
an olive tree sapling (really a young tree), dead with heat or frost.
Lacking, it crumbled under the cold sun, wild oats flourishing
around its throat. I felt its death and wished tears would flow

from black springs within me. That's worth an argument, Walt Whitman,
and though I am just one of many addressing you at any given time,
few here from the valley would hold you accountable in any way.
My great-grandmother was born in Boston, where the third edition

of *Leaves of Grass* was published — 1860 and she a young woman
with a ship to catch, the Antipodes anxious on her event horizon.
Through her you'll be held to account at Jam Tree Gully, the gnats
busy about manure and grass, flies erupting from echidna scats
where red ants have eaten far into that white-ant silence.

We drove past the salt hindquarters of Wheatlands with friends
      and admired the reclamation in passing: now Timber Creek
where my cousin Ken farms with his family. I was quite close to him
      as a kid but we rarely cross paths now. As the crow flies
(and it does) we are probably 75 ks apart: Jam Tree Gully to Timber
      Creek. Each particle of distance an intensity of separation.
There are still links but they're uncharged. Whitman at *his* Timber Creek
      threaded other lifeforms into his tapestry — the pond a beginning
or an end to his creek. But out of the salt, three creeks begin, making
      salt slices and chambers where old roots once gave infrastructure
to tubes and tunnels, fibre optic of the transition from fresh to saline
      marches, those tints and filaments long beneath awaiting release.
What residues are left from boyhood, obsessed over by Whitman,
      for me a bemusement at closeness that filters how we interpret
the handings-on, next generations (and next and next) of creatures
      that overlap here and there — how we view *their* being
and our being, what makes role and presence. The essence of survival.
      It's the drying that alters decorum — the sharp light off
crystalline structures in segments between trees, holding ground.
      Not a use memory is often put to — in realtime you are there
and I am here, and similar dirt and stone and latitude are beneath
      our feet. But at Jam Tree Gully we have some elevation,
though feeding the same river, the same system, as those creeks.
      Observation that is itemising isn't enough, true. But lists
have to be made and the data brought into play for the benefit of all —
      mutual aid. The critic who says there's not much philosophical
depth to commentaries on atheism and agnosticism should examine
      a square metre or even a square inch beneath their feet
and take note. Camping at Hathaways, the cold night wanting in, I
      probably confided in Ken — I recall he talked of plains

native Americans in the mid-nineteenth century. A model for life.

The salt wastes were his wide sky spaces. He rode a horse.

We drank water from aluminium canteens from the army surplus store

and the taste is still with me, though it impairs memory.

From Timber Creek to Jam Tree Gully, I will hear you if you recall

loudly, as unlikely as it needs be, the same moon over salt.

INVERSIONS

See signs of the tawny frogmouth during the lightest hours
but don't hear it at night. Winter habits of cloud, darkness, light?

Ute runs along the railway line — silent as the devil.
Wheat train smashing its way up the valley where there are no tracks.

Sidetracked by Gabriel Fauré's *Requiem* it looks bright sunshine
regardless of clouds; air crisp and fresh and unspoiled; poison
         containers stacked high at the tip.

The wind's sudden (and brief) howl really sounds more like a vacuum
sucking its breath in at the point of asphyxiation, equating with anomaly.

It's easy to say that there's nothing splendid about this isolation.
But then again, I was telling Tim about the value of platitudes

and how conservative the rowdies (in truth) are around here: ensuring
quotas of ammo and poisons are maintained, wanting their meals cooked

by their wives and girlfriends and mothers at the same time every day,
in the predictable ways. Cold beer always stocked in the fridge.

Sun skink sheltering on skin of log — winter sun hesitant and tardy and its
   appearance
makes the insides of the log (the hollow) less appealing —hibernation
   ambiguous.
       No gameplay is benign.

Always awaiting weather fronts — one of *substance* expected overnight. The first
stirrings of breeze, soon to play ducks & drakes with objects light and less secure.
       A time of rearrangement almost on us.

True, I suffer emptiness and reassure myself or insist there's no time for navel-gazing in such an ancient part of the planet, knowing change won't sweep it clean. Spiritual desolation?

EMPATHY OF SPACE: A SATIRE?

Space is nothing without empathy.

Intrusion is a resentment of rusty nails and snakebite (an equation
that collapses with the most gentle fatigue test). Love thy neighbour:
they get further and further away, the further out you go.
Do the stretch: makes you think.
                                    The jiddy jiddy follows or stalks me
in fog and darkness.
                        I work best at twilight, evening star out,
sunset's nimbus almost gone, collecting kindling
slightly damp from evening dew to dry under shelter
overnight. It makes sense at that time, if it's quiet —
void of gunshot and machinery — the jiddy jiddy and night creatures
making sounds for their own purposes.
Space collects around all of us, a membrane
we press against with lesser and greater certainty.
I have my second waking of the day, and it is the deepest
waking. The hurt less visible, darkness immense
and beyond damage
                        in some ways, many ways.

A nightbird dashed itself against this window (page, glass, elsewhere)
last night: twice. I rushed outside and heard a surprised, sickly chant
wheeling downhill, as from treetop to treetop, a skerrick
of light taken from the edges of blinds, the lure, the unbalancing:
areas of low combustion on the sun's surface, the creeping dark
at the poles, but the drenching of space is solar activity:
in such contradiction the nightbird's reaching for the corona

of the window and the complex, infinite physics of adaptation
when evolution is under the hammer, the sparking raining out
from the tests, the needs, the breeding out
to make do with whatever surfaces, long drag around the sun,
the many gods it hauls up.

      A crisis of kookaburras plugging
into the deadwood extensions of the great eucalypt above the house,
fully-charged and sabotaging copyright and greed through sharp,
expeditious beaks. That's at the time of wood-collecting,
in the spaces of activity following all events.

At this point of smoke and noise, of sculptural irresponsibility
on hillsides — gouged-out, scraped, refaced — the urge to look out
is conflicted, maybe more than ever, their inner spaces summoned
in a version of multi-directional gravity not yet named or copyrighted
but certainly discovered, long lived with. Or are there names
that don't carry over, lost or suppressed or safely hidden away
in aspects of those very spaces? The movement away isn't rapid,
no case of sharp departures, it's a dilution, a figurative or actual loss
of memory, all electrical and cellular, the chemicals of belonging
working together to keep it real, keep it natural. The reconstructions
of the ancient Greek world in the disharmony of industrio-chemical
brute forces. Now, again, who could ever call any of it nature?
What was it?
It never was.

    Into the drifts of persecutions the birds
with legs longer than wings fly — overhead now — passing,
passing by — follow them, follow them, tail feathers needles
of compasses running contrary to the devices we've rigged

to make direction as we want it.

                         Transitional objectivity
leaving us home free?

                         The disturbed clouds make negatives
of the days.

              Letting noise in is an act of filtering
each denomination, each pitch of bird conversation; that allows
me to get past the machinery preparing the 'Highlands' loop
for the thanatos thrill-seeking of the annual Targa rally: the eco-
haters' excursion into sublimity, a velocity-*enfer*.

                                        Action poétique
once had 'Poètes de la Réunion' *and* Ed Dorn and Jerome Rothenberg
on the same cover and we can link this to the air rushing indoors
from the open window with the parts-per-million of everything
and its vectors.

              Or the easing of anxiety notwithstanding the rough-
shod brutality of the rally incursion, the hood lifted from the eyes
to show trees and animals and rocks aren't bones of the wastes,
even humorously (a nervous laughter), that relief is no responsibility
for poetry outside what you will write, need to write in the high
pH psychic trauma, the carbon dioxide breakdown of landscape.

PUFFBALL OUTBREAK

Speckled outcome of breakup once skin's tolerance
pre-ordained volume has been reached and breached,
or potato-skin purity eyeless and taut with beneath-
surface though these domes are so *above*, whatever rhizomes
in expression of *underneath*; or eggs of damnation
with interior compaction of dispersal writ in exterior,
temporal agony, constrained not much longer,
though among the nine in two square metres,
semi-shaded at most times on winter days,
the deflated forerunners, the fate of primordial
firsts, vanguards to wilt in the same way as latecomers:
in their prime, bold as explosions, as lush as a beautiful
pregnancy; or, dubious domes — *no*, pernicious domes —
of lookout and surveillance (steady, steady . . . anticipate surprise)
of radar balloons midwest, up in the Chapman Valley,
where we were a few weeks ago collecting similes
to reconstitute here at Jam Tree Gully. Mantra it,
swallow it whole, more than a placebo, healthkick it,
but never consume puffballs from here or Geraldton
or anywhere as your dreams of ripeness won't work
here or there. And though you'll read and hear
they're edible at the point when interiors are fleshy,
before the murky green dust-storm of spores,
don't be fooled. They know you're hungry
in too many ways to count. Resist the urge,
take pre-emptive action. Look at them closely
with clear consciences. They will respect you for this.

UNIVERSAL TRANSLATOR

Exposed to the elements, this typewriter clicks
in time with syrinxes at full throttle, a driving
out of tunes' concordance, a 'universal translator',
expression of joy now the rally cars and their blinkered
drivers have gone. Their absence is a boon, a tuning
fork — five birdsongs entwine and are laid down here —
think rhythm of the keys, think octaves, think trills.
Finger exercises to work jam tree blossom, the yellowing
of the blue and green world, far more intense rev count.

What soul was dragged on the slow train across
the island continent? What Endymion-memory of poets
I cherish? What bits taken to recite, the canon coming to bits
with the jostling of tracks on concrete sleepers, Nullarbor clarity
and its contaminants; it owns the fallout now, whatever
the cause. And what souls brought back as sparks
in the grate kept warm by Tracy, whom I love. And Tim,
ten years and seventh months, counting the facts, the stats,
whom I love equally. Roo-prints in the wet soil: it has rained

here though the prints came late and stuck, maybe over
earlier prints. The shaken, translated soul: volatile, it returns.

It's Flying Ant Day at Jam Tree Gully.
An early spring, if that's what we can call it now.
We've already well and truly been sprung.
The virgin queens are guided from their bunkers
onto hillock runways, tended by their vested interests
in indirect and distant and over-familiar ways
(also the males with wings and exploding-genitalia-
in-waiting); the bright day flights begin with a flurry.
Launches are spectacular and we all watch, not even slightly
voyeur in the sheer wonder of colonial thanatos and birth-
of-nation stuff. The frenzy of an often busy empire
is the highpoint of history and ritual and belief,
this, too, is spirituality and sublimity on collision
course — and intervention is reaching into periphery
to lift the straying caterpillar frantically segmenting
across the priesthood and temples to Artemis, out of the dark
tunnels they come — it's too intense to focus, even to be
swarm — out of Hecate's chambers into 'conditions are right'
glibness of human watchfulness, curiosity and fear.
All marriages end in death, and our marriage night
is always to come, or lived over, or quietly recounted.
The breaking of the moon's meniscus in the glory of the sun.
Day and night becoming one, blinding by the light,
wing-glinting-rip into air, into the layers of kin.

RILKE ON RODIN VIA JAM TREE GULLY
AFTER LATE WINTER RAIN

'Living human beings didn't speak to him in those years. Stones spoke.'

'These pieces retain at midday the mysterious shimmer
emanated by white objects at twilight.'

'The air that comes to this stone abandons its will;
it doesn't pass beyond this piece to other things;
it embraces stone, hesitates, lingers, and lives in it.'
RILKE ON AUGUSTE RODIN *(translated by Daniel Slager)*

When they uprooted the granites to make the arena —
Zone of flatness and nothingness — the square for the circle
Of horses, to control their way of moving — *exercise* —
The great satire of possession came into play, shire
Permissions in pocket (after all, it's not a structure
Above the surface, but a levelling-off). Those stone
Asides are the sculpture of 'progress', a jibe at the art
Of causality, of the found. In a photo with the light
(dependent on air) working its contrasts, it is made art
and relevant to the sensitive, to the perceptive, to the *arty*.

The tumble and fall and repositioning of granites to locate
Micro-ecologies works in the replenishing we impose;
In applying what Rilke observed in the boar-snout
(Camille Claudel residue), lecherous eyes, and imaging
Hands of Rodin, to decontextualise, to misattribute,
To consider Balzac with an erection, is *all* to those partying
In the hilltop enclave — whose strains we are battered by

On weekends, the moulding of space through sound.
The night revelries reverberate, sharp white light;
Agitated hands struggle with prayer and work.

Is this merely the complaint of a jaded neighbour,
Or a genuine case of idiocy — imbeciles and fools
To the gathering — or righteous indignation? Rights
Of quiet enjoyment, of peace and quiet? Granite explosion,
Fate of all stone flicked off the arena, the circus? The big
Thumbs down? Conjure Kavanagh's fool in rural Ireland,
All clans with their roots, the gasping revival, bulldozers
Upending standing stones worshipped in peaty soil.
Here, loam harbours organisms that enhance and damage
Your sense of permanence, air shimmering with riot.

HALLELUJAH

I wrote this title
after listening to *The Messiah*.
Then news came of a friend's
stage-four palliative treatment.

He said, 'It is what it is'.
And that's it. But what is *it*?
It is everything and more
than what it is.

Hallelujah
goes so many ways.
Hallelujah
takes a leaf from the book.

VEREY VEREY LIGHTS

Alien bonfires
across the valley
flare into a tempering
night sky, splinters
raining down on our house,
scratching the tin roof,
stabbing into wood and dirt.

Or are *we* the aliens
those incendiarists
hope to illuminate,
burn out?

STRAW POLL

The yellow rain of wattle pollen
foams on gravel, it falls at a slant
to bunch up and aerate: the interruption
of passage, of flow; fizzing, erupting.

What 'sexual specifications', Bachelard,
in the alchemy of loadstone pollen, dispersal
of blossom, breakdown of structure? Reproduction.
Or gratification in under-pressure scenarios,

deployment of data, fracture of witness.
All perpetuities collapse in the froth,
buzzed by insects who will plunge
into the yellow pith, excrescence

of sex. Their sex relies on it. All
of it. Endgame, to ride roughshod
the inadequacies of perception:
sexual organs flung round all

over the place, pollen on our shoes,
stamen extravaganza, pollinator ultra,
wrecking our heads. Headfucked.
And now, wild oats losing their seed,

their sex parts long past, or is this
the primacy of sex: the seed: the falling,
the caught-by-the-breeze, the stigma
of traditional ways? And then stalks

yellowing to straw in the haze of wattles,
voting with their deaths in the busy
picture of rural vegetation. No consensus
of the waving-in-the-wind variety,

the Godbotherers and shooters,
motoring enthusiasts and family firsts,
the soul-collecting and the brave
imprimaturs of public pollination.

Straw grows more brittle as heat
kicks in — washed, dried, bleached —
powdering in the lightest sea-breeze
struggling inland where people

also live, gasping for air,
lamenting their allergies.

NATIVE CUTWOOD DEFLECTS
COLONIAL HUNGER

Why 'raspberry jam tree'? Acacia acuminata. Mungart.
The guilt of cutwood? Its smell, its bloody show?
And that colourist's jam envy, the lust for ropes
of raspberry. Fence-posts sturdy and hardy
and doused in creosote: to stand alone
in termitesville. The sweetness turns rust.
And burnt offerings unless dried right through —
say for a year on the pile. Hot as hell to fire.
Nothing comes cost-free, we hear — those layers
of its dozen years a demonstration in history
as accumulation. Collective survey of occupation:
the real *corps de ballet*, the shrubby scenery,
bulldozed on roadsides. Ring-a-ring-a-rosy.
All those brandings. Emblem of *our town*
that would miss no more than our rates.
'High turnover' region. Think raspberry
jam on white damper, think coals of fires.
The meagre shade for sheep and cattle
and the denial of 'unproductive' animals.
Nuisances. Saw deep into rough bark,
showered in pollen. Unholy fires
at the end of winter; and all that premonition,
all those seeds with snow in their bellies,
snow that can't fall from this faraway sky.
So overwhelmingly familiar to me.
No Old Country raspberry homesickness.
Just an inkling of anthocyanin pigments.
Why 'raspberry jam tree'? Acacia acuminata. Mungart.

THE SWARM'S GENERATING AND
DEGENERATING ELLIPSE

In the warp of bees clustering
swarm on jam tree foliage,
hooked in a tear drop
overheating with its reaction,
arrhythmic heart seeking
otherworld entry
via cathodal leaves and sprig,
shaping to our eyes as demijohn
then wineskin, a collusive upending,
collective concentration, queen
of body politic a furtive tippler,
godhead in her manna, hotline
to afterworld to stun and stagger
and then be gone; though now
at full tilt, powering out
on journey to infrastructure,
guts of the state, the swarm shifts
shape to form its own plans,
its beginnings and ends,
transitory maps incontinent as empires,
passing ephemerally into the fervent
oval with quadrant sliced away,
semi-major and semi-minor
axis declaration:
all that pettifogging
barnstorming
gatekeeping

dossier-drawing secret outings
and grandslam exposés
buzzed away. This is it, mate,
transitional as fatalism.

ON MIZEN

PENINSULA, IRELAND

ORANGE 1962 MASSEY FERGUSON
TRACTOR, CORTHNA

I know that tractor. I have driven a blue version
many times in the Avon Valley. Not as hilly as here,
but in the wet things still got boggy, and hard work
was a catchcry. Built the same year I was built,
orange required less gestation time. I was birthed
early in sixty-three, probably around the same time
blue arrived at Fremantle Harbour.

Orange belongs to the landlady's father,
eighty-two and insisting 'she' will see
him out. The life they've shared together,
not mutually exclusive, but room
in the family unit. Almost a sisterly
affection, but not quite. It might be Mother,
but that place is filled eternally,
a blessing of the fields.

Machine grows into personality
but it's no case of a dog and its master.
Out into the fields of Corthna
orange sucks in the Atlantic fogs:
factory and farm, longevity,
and maybe if the lid on the exhaust
breaks off, I can suggest a jam tin
wired over to keep rain out,
let the exhaust free into the idyll.

IMAGINE THIS WILD SEA FROM
JAM TREE GULLY

I am in a hot room at Jam Tree Gully
Looking out on this wild sea, wind
Battering the double-glazed windows.
Bays and islands, channels and harbours.
A collection of Mizen Head oral histories
Collected by schoolchildren: grandparents
Remembering parents remembering
The many ways of death, closing up house
And dying together, the fever in one bed.
We are having nightmares. The burial pits
Underwrite our assisted passage, our blow-
Back presence. In this hot room at Jam Tree
Gully, I am smelling the cut brittle grass,
Recording the appearance of bearded dragons.
Year after year, a mapping to end all maps,
Picking our way through names imposed
By our gaunt and famished ancestors,
Trying to reset the geography, the compass.
In this hubris, a collage forms and a new,
Wordless book is made. Ink runs before
Words are set, the swell so fierce, swarm
Of wild bees from the storm-damaged tree,
From the quakes resonating across the planet.

WHEATBELT AND WEST CORK
COLONIAL DIEGETIC

Tonsured stones \ convict church   Tonsured stones / famine church
Prison-grotesque   Halloween emaciation masks
Massacre sites   Bodies 'coffinless' crammed in pits
Exfoliate granite discards   Moss and lichen on copper scars
Xenophobia on roads too narrow for visitors, walled and rutted long
occupation unwinding from spools despite erasure doesn't cross-reference
plumes of carcinogens flowing from chimneys in less 'green' towns.

Smokeless coal and peat makes haloes about crows cawing into sealed rooms;
think of Zola on the continent, the truck of bourgeois emancipation, think
conspiracy of military and locals counting costs of clean breath, think

the Lisbon earthquake and a beach thrown up on Mizen Head — Barley
Cove the scene of sandcastles and tonnes of cocaine; in the wheatbelt speed
is burning classrooms smashing asbestos panels; victims of berserkers.
Odour of fossil fuels   Old world disinterred
Burning words   Munitions fires
Tonsured stones / famine church   Tonsured stones \ convict church

WHITE QUARTZ OF THE DROMBEG
STONE CIRCLE

Fixating on a white quartz
seam in the grey standing stone
west of the recumbent stone
the megalithic becomes
geological; sunlight
in late November is free
of conjecture and ritual,
of blood and burial, teeth
of the portal, a desire
to offset cars, cameras,
roads, tractors, contrails, the lust
for electricity; white
quartz is not an uncommon
rock back at Jam Tree Gully,
largish chunks broken up by
heavy machinery, now
crystals in the schematics
of geomorphology.
Some come and hear the banshee.
Some leave quickly because 'bad
vibes' emanate; others will
believe they have made contact
with a primal truth, accessed
a subtle technology
far less damaging than their
arrival or departure.
On one stone a hair-clip rests,
simple object of complex
manufacture. The motive?

Such compulsions of white quartz
follow the sun. Tomorrow
a hair-clip will be called for.

REINTRODUCTION

Atlantic winds are cutting Mizen Head,
wheedling hollows and cracks in slate hills,
altering vocal cords, shaping words.
I have been struggling to identify a large
bird of prey we saw in County Kerry
a few weeks ago, as intense and bothering
as a floater in the eye, it lured my sight
from the road, from hairpin bends,
sheep raddled with rival farmers' claims.
It rose where rocks rise quickly from the sea
to make mountains, and flew alone.
Back home, wedge-tailed eagles command
the valley, and are reference points
for conflict of interest. Into their spirals
and talons and beaks and wingspans
are ascribed pro- and anti- attitudes
to hunting rights in national parks
and reserves, the dominance of mining
companies and fly-in fly-out metabolism;
to the planting of genetically modified crops,
use of Roundup along roadsides,
clearing of remnant bushland,
and quid pro quo of human-induced
climate change, on what *use* non-domesticated
creatures are to the district's prosperity. The New
State of Nature. There are those who would
shoot eagles out of the sky — 'killers
of lambs' who would 'take human babies
if they could' — and then those who make them
symbol of all that is lost and what remains.

Pathetic fallacy and even noble savagery
are woven into these Symbolists' arguments,
which strive to articulate against the flow,
just want eagles left to their own devices.
The failure of arguments semiotically
and philosophically is neither here nor there:
no harm is meant to anyone or anything,
and we've got to take the Symbolists at their word.
At least they're not poisoning or shooting
as others do when they lampoon and deride
'protected species' status as greenies' jargon.
What brings me to rhetoric in the lyric is a picture
my mother sent this morning of a road-sign replete
with shotgun-blast puncturing, photographed
from behind (the sign itself is away from the sun —
all we have is the cratering from a narrow
spread of pellets that didn't burst through
but went close), a reflective silver-backing
of the sun semi-perforated, an irruption
of binary data that speaks a brutal code.
In the blue sky behind and above, in the distance,
a wedge-tailed eagle is angling away.
Caught in the photo, or catching the photo;
to spread its propaganda? Having its way?
I transcribe 'home', 'brutality', 'vulnerability',
'threat', 'loss', and even an absent signifier
from this. I can feel the heat in the sign,
the sky, the shot. Cooler up there where
the eagle is, but closer to the sun. Here and now,
unable to identify the bird of prey we saw
in the rocky places of Kerry, I comb books
and discover white-tailed eagles
were reintroduced into that county

some years ago, that they once bred there
as late as the first years of the twentieth century,
victim of modernity and linguistics. Since
reintroduction, when many sheep farmers
protested vehemently, some eagles have been
poisoned. I write my famine ancestors. I write
their passage to the south-west of Australia.
They were Carlow and Wicklow people.
They may have seen vagrant white-tailed eagles
up there, in the mid-nineteenth century,
during the famine, but probably not.
Too inland, too high, too far, too rare.
They would have seen wedge-taileds, surely,
soon after their arrival in Nyungar country.
Foresters and farmers. My grandfather,
head state forester, was based at Gleneagle.
Eagles' aviatronics over 'his' forest, his 'realm'.
As a child, my father gave eagles names
to forget the names he'd been told. There are
no simple answers. Wing and hand, feather
and bone, rock and vegetation, the tangling
of speech and thought. The adoration
of raptors. Their demise and reintroduction.
Mum has labelled the photo 'sign with shots'.
She doesn't need to mention the eagle.
Barthes' *Mythologies* is on her shelves
and she is thrilled her grandson
is learning Irish. It is almost summer
there. Here, winter is closing in.

FALLING INTO CAPE CLEAR ISLAND

You are walking briskly back down Ardmanagh Road towards Anchor
    Lodge,
A driving wind over your shoulder picking up traces of copper from the
    heights,
When you are lifted by a gust and carried over Schull Harbour out into the
    bay,
Falling into Cape Clear Island from the foot of the Old Red Sandstone
    range.

Distance is nothing as vertigo unravels space, seams unthread from stone,
A dark sky suddenly clear, macadam soft as wet peat, a fish at your ear;
Feeling unwell, this is how you piece it all back together, draw on 'flying
    dreams',
Falling into Cape Clear Island from the foot of the Old Red Sandstone
    range.

You might fall all the way to Jam Tree Gully, a trick of curvature, logic of
    sphere,
But it's outside imagining, your feet looking for immediate traction, the
    fear;
Off a school vocabulary list, you lift *sa bhaile*, which is where you will land,
Falling into Cape Clear Island from the foot of the Old Red Sandstone
    range.

Not long after take-off you gain a bird's-eye view of a slate cottage, broken
Down to chimney and two walls, and witness a crown of moss and ferns, self-
Sufficient as much as anywhere else, and you transfer this knowledge to
    speech,
Falling into Cape Clear Island from the foot of the Old Red Sandstone
    range.

So exclaiming as you sweep over the water, Mount Gabriel your ceiling,
You become ash on the wind, cryo-burnt offering, scattered to the here and
   now;
But heritage has set you this launch place, appointed this unknown drop
   zone,
Falling into Cape Clear Island from the foot of the Old Red Sandstone
   range.

ELECTRIC ROCOCO RECOLLECTIONS OF
JAM TREE GULLY FROM AFAR

From the upper south-east window
the cross on the church is stark —
light-globes mark its outline, contrast
the twilit harbour. It wants more
out of symmetry than is on offer.

Tomorrow, the Guru is going over
to Jam Tree Gully to clear the gutters
of tinder-dry leaves. They congest
without style, embellish with urge,
the pragmatism of making a growth
medium: in summer easterlies red dust
falls as the true rain of modernity
and tumbles into the leafy bed
already set in aluminium conduits.
If fire comes, a stray ember or spark
will make rocket fuel of this process.

No ember or spark has come
to ignite dry-leaf coffins;
No ember or spark has come
to make heat that can melt metal;
No ember or spark has come
to leave soft beds of grey ash;
No ember or spark has come
to the gutters, though it might;
No ember or spark has come
but you will clear leaves in case.

Deadzone is where dead trees
lose their shadows, fail to flower
shade. All that brocade of less-
than-light vanquished, all design
levelled out. As pat as a hot bed
of ash, the terror of boot-prints,
the flickers of flame that will
burn the dead again and again.

But don't think fear has ground
art out of the picture: down the road
a house done up like Fred and Wilma
Flintstone's: a pebbledash of pride,
a B52s/Koons in-joke with raised
flowerpots for alien species,
raised beyond the grinding
teeth of kangaroos.

With double-glazed windows
sealed to the 'beautiful view',
breathing stale, trapped air
to escape the cascades of coal smoke,
I make memories of what hasn't
happened far away at Jam Tree Gully.
Anxiety governs the use of proper nouns,
though I frequently listened to Rococo
composers, their dancing feet tacky
with Baroque foundations. François
Couperin tinkled galante in the background
(I first heard Mum play the harpsichord
when I was too young to picture
the rural as quaint). Playful
in the background. That 'who

gives a damn while the peasants
starve' music. As if I could latch
on to the fertilisation image: an earth
hungry for the starving. Here, the famine
pits, and there, plasterwork repainted
brightly in colonial houses, those standouts.

From the upper south-east window
the cross on the church is stark —
light-globes mark its outline, contrast
the twilit harbour. It wants more
out of symmetry than is on offer.

It's obvious to think of Fragonard's *The Swing*
at times like these: those layers of garment.
A swing from a tree at Jam Tree Gully
would bring down the branch it hung
from: termites working strength illusory.
And even if it swung for a while,
you'd need to wear camouflage
lest shooters grew attracted
to the moving target.

Hear 'Les Lis naissans' . . .
Hear 'Les Barricades Mystérieuses' . . .
Hear the clarity of electricity,
the warmth of synapses,
the global chatter: grey wagtail,
golden whistler, maybe
the tek tek in the cirques
of La Réunion . . .

As my baroque infrastructure
collapses into glimpses, the ironies
of being attacked by a neighbour
who is angry with the effete,
the exquisite channels of death — gullies —
formed by angry run-off sluicing the hillside,
the filigree of spray downhilling
from Shire 'weed prevention',
neighbours flourishing, those sweet
rococo rememberings, the cuts
of the harpsichord; ooze, pout, flourish,
flare, flutter, festoon, leisure, pleasure . . . warmth.
The blood-warmth of paradox,
listening through light of sun on hills,
decadence of feet up on the verandah,
fire in the belly of the world.

No ember or spark has come
to ignite dry-leaf coffins;
No ember or spark has come
to make heat that can melt metal;
No ember or spark has come
to leave soft beds of grey ash;
No ember or spark has come
to the gutters, though it might;
No ember or spark has come
but you will clear leaves in case.

Consider the radioactive spill
at Ranger uranium mine in Kakadu:
'mud, water, ore and acid'.

Consider praising the mining giant, Rio Tinto!
Roll it over again: 'mud, water, ore and acid'
(got that from a mining journo's report).
Mantra it: 'mud, water, ore and acid'.

Consider the photo Mum sent yesterday
of the bloody and inflamed sunset
beside Walwalinj — replete
with burnt bush, houses, cars, animals.

Consider the photos she sent of magpies
stepping into a bowl of cold water
placed on the verandah, of the *cold-blooded*
flocking to the cool: bungarras drinking,
bungarras dunking one foot at a time,
a rococo gesture in forty-six centigrade
(in the shade) heat.

Consider leaves in the gutter at Jam Tree Gully.

Consider the Guru wanting to cut away saplings
whose leaning sheds volatile eucalyptus leaves
into the repositories.

Consider the frequency of storms where I am now,
where I am with Tracy and Tim and locals
who smart at the weather, the Atlantic churning it up —
restless, confused, asymmetrical, affronted
by its own premature senility.

Consider Wallace Stevens swinging anchorless, beheaded:
polite, insular, interior, almost comfortable.

Consider the coal smoke rolling out onto sea,
settling as film, stretching across water to Atomic France,
home of the Rococo and gorgeous reactors.

No ember or spark has come
to ignite dry-leaf coffins;
No ember or spark has come
to make heat that can melt metal;
No ember or spark has come
to leave soft beds of grey ash;
No ember or spark has come
to the gutters, though it might;
No ember or spark has come
but you will clear leaves in case.

From the upper south-east window
the cross on the church is stark —
light-globes mark its outline, contrast
the twilit harbour. It wants more
out of symmetry than is on offer.

CROSSING THE IRISH SEA FROM ROSSLARE
TO FISHGUARD BETWEEN STORMS

Roulis et tangage, heavy swell to pitch a portent,
the sailing between storms — yesterday a Force 10
passage, an engine-room strain against landbridge,
a walk across to make stone-age reckoning with new
human-space, to walk now the sea a scoop
of mercury, of radiation, of language-suspended
solutions. Some call it the 'vomitorium', others
look over the stern into full-moon darkness-failure,
a wake of gulls to cross the heaving water. Walking
down from the hotel to harbour in the dead cold air
I heard the cordylines furiously alive, their click-a-clack
rustle that'd shred the knuckles, their reassuring
hustle in recollection. From the deep Antipodean
hedging bets against the inclination to warmer hearths,
those brazen coals, that smoking funnel. So I send
a message to Tom down in Australia, his heat sensors
working tones of vegetation against all burnings,
the rough and ready summer, the *roulis et tangage*
of apprehension, a storm that will stop all voyages
at our tails, all instruments bent to its emphasis.

JAM TREE GULLY STOPOVER
CONSIDERED FROM SCHULL

Stephen and Dzu stop over
at Jam Tree Gully to check on the house
on their way back to Bookara.

They arrange wrought-iron chairs
beneath shade-cloth to have lunch.
Later, I will say to Mum, 'I hope

they checked for redbacks.' Mum says
she asked the same thing and Stephen
responded, 'Redbacks don't bother me.'

That's true. They never have.
He let them crawl over his hands
as a child, took them to school

to make webs in his desk. As an
interpolation, I might add that he
was bitten by a python the other day

trying to lift it from the road:
six puncture-marks in his wrist
the hospital didn't know how to treat.

I know Stephen and Dzu would have
seen or heard a dozen species of bird
while they ate, discussing the valley.

It makes you listen in a different way,
their being not long back from Malaysia
and still drawing comparisons. Stephen

has to work tomorrow with a full shed
of sheep to shear. The imam in Perth
spoke of respect and he will extend

that to all living things, as will Dzu. They
are part of the Jam Tree Gully focus — looking
it over, wondering how far away we are.

The redbacks won't bother them
and the shade-cloth will not delete the sun.
I hope they know the water from the tank

isn't fit to drink — just for washing. So long
away, so far from here. But I step in while
transcribing and it becomes artefact.

JAM TREE GULLY

ENVOYS

GATEKEEPERS

Arriving home in the pitch dark
before the Milky Way floods
the moonless night with pinpoint accuracy,
we find a pair of roos either side
of the crossover, lit-up in the headlights,
coy eye-to-eye, turning slightly away
to protect their retinas, allowing
maculas to take in the writing of car,
bluemetal, gravel, fence, blue-black grass.
I step out to open the gate and they
move off either side, equidistant, balanced
in the shadows, peripheral to the operation
of opening. I return to Tracy and Tim
and we talk it over, then drive on through,
sentinels neither allowing or denying,
but switching the side-on glance to full
intake, absorption of our light and its risks,
the consequences of grazing where people
have so long been away, where new rules
will come into play, but they'll be let
go about their business and we will too.

HERMIT'S SONG

a version after Kuno Meyer's 1911 translation from the ninth
century Ériu (in *Selections from Ancient Irish Poetry*)

Spirits of the land, God arching overhead but never above, I desire
No more than to be part of this house at Jam Tree Gully, the environs.

I have peace in the company of weebills and red-capped robins,
And when the rains come and wash through Bird Gully I am replete.

I lament the burning-out of the flooded-gum grove below,
And offer shelter to the wildlife that fled to higher ground.

Even when the sun drops west over the hills, I acknowledge
Its rays curling colours along the granites — I own none of this

But share it with a network of living things, the soul-fabric
Of geckoes and acacias, my partner and our son, all of their ways.

We don't go out to pray, but each knows the weight of words,
Each listens for the call and response of other creatures.

Three of us inside with spiders and stray ants, while outdoors
The complexity of crosstalk and overlay, of loss and gain.

Eagles have been absent for a year now and we fear for them
And ourselves. But scripture is each stroke in dirt, needlewasp on flyscreen.

Inside or out, we are all of this house built here at a cost — though we've
Kept below the height of the bush, hidden by something greater.

I would reduce ownership to clear breath and that silence shared
With grazing kangaroos, the determined echidna, waking nightbirds.

It's enough, though it's hard to make a living so removed — to drink the
water.
Sometimes it's hardest to express gratitude when alone. A few others help.

Growth of trees is measured against the red shed,
loud edifice now clear of old hay and dung,
though still cluttered with rolls of fencing wire
extracted and collated from the block, and tools
for keeping the grass down, and paraphernalia
for running the pump, and the air pump itself,
its hoses reaching out under the red walls
to outposts, wells sunk deep through hills,
sucking at the conflicted water table, though now
the pump is at 'stop', having rarely lifted beyond
dead slow ahead. The red shed shines in reports
of its discomfort, its red entanglement with a killer
sun, its ventilator moving when the breeze
will barely lift a leaf on the York gums towering
nearby. Bees have been attracted to its gutters
but don't stick around, it's *that* forbidding;
they prefer the trees whose growth we track.
The red shed barely knows itself as waste,
believing its divine purpose: shade to insects,
pupae clinging to sundry items, snuggled
into the dirt floor. I don't agree with most
of its choices, and though lingering in its cave
even when away, a niche or recess in my mind
concentrating on the scene at hand, I don't
worship its structural integrity. I have wondered . . .
a copy of Veblen's *The Theory of the Leisure Class*
flapping its yellow brittle leaves when the great
sliding door is wrenched open, a copy
just flung there on the floor, this sentence
underlined: 'expresses itself in some form

of conspicuous waste.' From memory
a 'spiritual' want languishes in the factory
where shed walls are rolled, or is that far
from the comfort zones of mansions
down in the city, offices of the Club
where red sheds are tossed back
with a drink of fine wine? Captains
of industry. *Conspicuous* behind
closed doors. The fencing wire,
the pump, the pupae, the pipes
snaking out into places where they
grow soggy with heat, then brittle
when the frosts come, cracking
their covenant, drawing nothing
from below even when the pump
is fired up, thirsty heart of the shed.

We see two palls of smoke as we head home to Jam Tree Gully
from Mum's place near York. One is thick and black and issuing
from a valley near Northam, the other past Clackline where wooded
hills edge wheatfields. Two of the three routes we might take.
We opt for the Clackline-Toodyay Road and guess that fire
is coming out of bush fringing the gaping mouth of the gravel pit
we've watched eat away the marri and jarrah trees over recent years.
Tracy sees helitacs flying through the smoke and we drive alongside
another helitac brooding beside a farm dam. Bushfire brigades
arrive from Toodyay and Bejoording and we wave to the crews
guessing we'll know some behind their yellow suits. I point to a header
still lopping ears of wheat as smoke plumes overhead, the tractor
with chaser-bin following in fits and starts to haul in what they can
before flame makes ashen windrows of the remaining crop. Tracy
says, 'Harvest in the shadow of fire . . .' and I remind her of my
motif from childhood, driving with Mum and Jackie and the other
kids through thick bush in the deep south when fire closed out
both sides and embers spat at the windows, we kids in the back
of the station wagon, a blanket around our noses, as the road
behind warped with the heat. This poem can't plant itself
in competition — no ancient laurels of Europeanism
with long lines and a heroic stance, no Pindaric ode
to the body perfect, to slake the ego's dreadful thirst.
No anonymity here. No sudden revelation of identity
to challenge doubters and sceptics, just a recollection
or last will and testament or simply a witness's account.

DOE WITH LARGE JOEY SNUGGLES AGAINST
THE HOT HOUSE AS FIRE APPROACHES

Her joey must be an *almost-permanently-*
outside-the-pouch-offspring, though with
the grey yellow muck of fire overhead
and our returning to the house, she guides
it headfirst into the only security she has
on offer — *outside* is immured.

The doe watches us carefully, edging
closer, sniffing the distance to the firefront,
closer to us and the house alongside which
she shelters — closer to us because we are all
creatures acting with caution and fear.

Too many roos have suffered in this burning-up
of country, out of all patterning, without
volition. She doesn't need to suffer in similes,
in analogies with inanimate objects, human devices.

We hear that the cause of this latest fire
is 'suspicious', and if the doe thinks it possible
for humans to undo things in that way,
don't expect complicity in the manufacture
of poems and artworks that diminish her,

that highlight the awkward weight
in her pouch, how difficult it is for her
to move away, the offspring peering out
over the rim in the fire's direction.

SAVING THE BOBTAIL MOTHER-TO-BE

A pregnant shingleback has got caught
in the old wire-mesh lining the verandah —
a leftover of the previous occupant's
dog days, the bullies she kept to drive off
strangers and kangaroos. Seven years later
this is one of the few traces of her presence,
though all presence goes deeper than signs —
the land is written over, never out.

A pregnant shingleback has got caught
in the old wire-mesh lining the verandah,
its triangular head through and one leg,
twisted in an attempt to move forward
then reverse, its swollen and spread belly
exposed to sharp-beaked crows, magpies,
and hook-clawed raptors. Tim calls us,
noting its distress — frantic rustling,
panting, blue tongue straining for speech.

A pregnant shingleback has got caught
in the old wire-mesh lining the verandah —
and I approach it from the front, wire-
snippers in hand, Tracy on the other side
of the divide. It hisses and spits at me,
desperate to break free. I move slowly,
ever so slowly, and as it closes its jaws
on my gloved hand and the Maun pliers,
I cut away mesh a few squares
from the square that traps it, hold

the shingleback with one hand and gently
shear away the corners of the square until
it is sprung free. Each movement matters,
each detail essential. *We are all in it
together* — a fusion of creatures and place.

A pregnant shingleback has got caught
in the old wire-mesh lining the verandah
and as it shucks the deadly collar, it
opens its mouth again, wider than its hinges,
and I am mesmerised by the beautiful blues
and pinks of its living interiority. And then
it half closes its eyes and rests, panting,
worn out with the fury, the anxiety, the trauma.

A pregnant shingleback has got caught
in the old wire-mesh lining the verandah.
It has probably passed through that square
many times but failed to judge its altered body,
maybe its first motherhood. It is part of the colony
burrowed into the sand under the cement
of the verandah. Know thyself. Know thy body.
But it's the body shared with live offspring —
the births close — any time, maybe later today.
This is nothing to do with me or Tim or Tracy
and everything to do with right place at right time.
Or are we entirely implicated, living in proximity,
co-signatories of ownership we all refuse but accept
by default? Our cold and warm blooded worlds.

A pregnant shingleback has got caught
in the old wire-mesh lining the verandah;

she is due and disorientated and left alone
she would die, hollowed out by time to skin
and bones, shingles and claws, the young
skeletons inside hers. Sermon, grace, science,
contact. *We are all in this together.* We'll say this
at least once or twice in our lives — in whatever
language, and with whatever tone or meaning.
Language is not rarefied in such moments —
nothing sings beyond the distressed gasp
and hiss and spit, the cutter rending wire.

WALKING THE FIREBREAKS

It's long after their first manifestation. They've *almost*
stayed the same as another summer has burnt over,

annealed or been disfigured by cruel easterlies — red
dust tissues samples. I walk them again — firebreaks

recuperating as *ground* — thinly — a splash of wild oat
seedlings, 'comforting' blanket of green almost everyone

waits for . . . but when the first flush is over, planning
how best to strip seasonal change away. One neighbour's

breaks stay bare in perpetuity, a stasis in poison, a magic window
into a next world where the spirit just *is*, without trimmings.

I walk 'ours' again, seeing the cracks growing out,
a difficult healing whose scars will shape next year's

incarnations, exponentially. And along the new-
skin of those cracks, puffballs — an impalpable code —

or field mushrooms breaking through, an underground
network not quite excised by the removal of yet

another top layer. I walk them again, with clean shoes
carrying nothing of the other lands I've visited:

no volcanic soil of La Réunion, no residues of Cork bogs,
no peat from the edges of Cambridgeshire fens, I walk

in the harsh light of shrinking days, of the tracks and stories
we have rerouted, changing inner and outer maps,

or rather thinking that we have. Firebreaks are so often
jumped — wide, straight, curved, steep — and we can't

create the colonial myth that will make them indelible.
They *will* grow over, and we will cut deeper next time round.